NICARAGUA

JENNIFER KOTT

MARSHALL CAVENDISH
New York • London • Sydney

Reference edition published 1995 by
Marshall Cavendish Corporation
2415 Jerusalem Avenue
P.O. Box 587
North Bellmore
New York 11710

Originated and designed by
Times Books International, an imprint of
Times Editions Pte Ltd

Printed in Singapore

Library of Congress Cataloging-in-Publication Data:
Kott, Jennifer.
    Nicaragua / Jennifer Kott.
       p. cm.—(Cultures Of The World)
    Includes bibliographical references and index.
    ISBN 1-85435-695-X : — ISBN 1-85435-690-9 (Series Set)
    1. Nicaragua—Juvenile literature. [1. Nicaragua.] I. Title.
II. Series.
F1523.2.K66 1994
972.85—dc20   94–28809
                          CIP
                          AC

Cultures of the World

Editorial Director	Shirley Hew
Managing Editor	Shova Loh
Editors	Elizabeth Berg
	Jacquiline King
	Dinah Lee
	Azra Moiz
	Sue Sismondo
Picture Editor	Susan Jane Manuel
Production	Anthony Chua
Design	Tuck Loong
	Ronn Yeo
	Felicia Wong
	Loo Chuan Ming
Illustrators	Anuar
	Chow Kok Keong
	William Sim
MCC Editorial Director	Evelyn M. Fazio
MCC Production Manager	Janet Castiglioni

INTRODUCTION

LOCATED IN THE political hotbed of Central America, Nicaragua is a beautiful tropical land with breathtaking mountain ranges and exotic rainforests. It has a long history of partisan hostilities, poverty, repression, and foreign occupation. Despite its problems, however, the country has a strong tradition of family unity and the courage and optimism to build a better future. Nicaraguans have worked hard to reduce illiteracy, racial injustice, and infant mortality, and they are continuing their fight to improve living conditions.

Perhaps what makes Nicaragua such an interesting nation is its people's determination to enjoy life—in spite of their troubles. With a rich tradition of poetry and a particular affinity for conversation, Nicaraguans are kind, generous, and insightful people. They enjoy celebrating numerous national and religious holidays, spending time with friends and family, and dancing and listening to music. Violence, economic problems, and disease still plague Nicaragua, but today the hope of a better tomorrow looks bright.

CONTENTS

One of many political wall murals in the cities.

CONTENTS

Years of fighting have left their mark on this bullet-riddled wall.

GEOGRAPHY

PICTURE AN AREA about the size of the state of New York, covered with forests, lakes, and mountains. Imagine long western and eastern coasts looking out onto the Pacific and Atlantic Oceans. This is how Nicaragua would look from an airplane flying over Central America. It is the largest country in the isthmus that lies between Mexico and South America, which is made up of seven countries, including Belize, Guatemala, Honduras, El Salvador, Costa Rica, and Panama.

To the north of Nicaragua lies Honduras, and to the south is Costa Rica. The western border is the Pacific Ocean, and to the east is the Caribbean Sea, which joins the Atlantic Ocean. In all, Nicaragua has about 560 miles of coastline. At 50,193 square miles, Nicaragua is a little bigger than Louisiana and a little smaller than North Carolina. Large areas of the country are uninhabited; most of its people are concentrated in the western region and in a few cities. The country's population per square mile is relatively thin compared to other Central American countries.

Left: **A volcano in Nicaragua's western volcanic area. Earthquakes and volcanic eruptions are frequent occurrences in Nicaragua.**

Opposite: **The Santiago Volcano near Masaya on the western coast. The top of the volcano can be reached by car.**

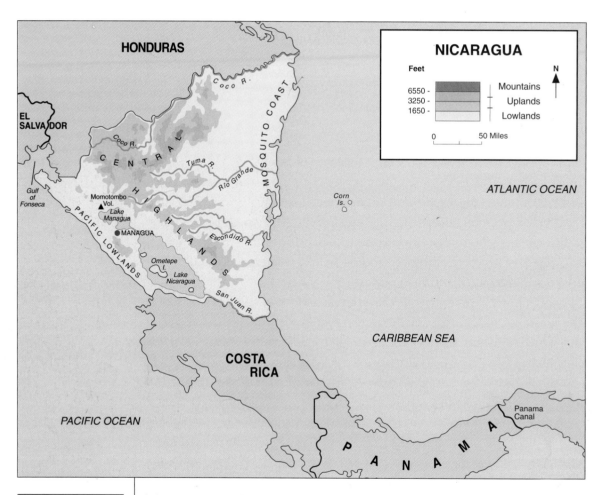

NICARAGUA

Feet

6550 -
3250 - | Mountains
1650 - | Uplands
          | Lowlands

0   50 Miles

HONDURAS

EL SALVADOR

Coco R.

Coco R.

Tuma R.

Río Grande

MOSQUITO COAST

Gulf of Fonseca

PACIFIC LOWLANDS

Momotombo Vol.

Lake Managua

MANAGUA

CENTRAL HIGHLANDS

Escondido R.

Ometepe I.

Lake Nicaragua

San Juan R.

Corn Is.

ATLANTIC OCEAN

CARIBBEAN SEA

COSTA RICA

PACIFIC OCEAN

PANAMA

Panama Canal

THREE REGIONS

Nicaragua is divided into three geographic regions: the western Pacific lowlands, the eastern Caribbean lowlands (also called the Mosquito Coast), and the central highlands. Each region has features and weather characteristics that differentiate it from other parts of the country.

PACIFIC LOWLANDS Three out of four Nicaraguans live in the western part of the country, between the Pacific coast and Lake Managua. Here, the land is good for growing things because it has been naturally fertilized over the years by ashes discharged from the area's many volcanoes. Many of the people who live here work on farms, but Nicaragua's three biggest

The Mosquito Coast is named after the Miskito Indians. When the Spanish name, Costa Miskito, was translated into English, it became Mosquito Coast, possibly because the area is infested with mosquitoes.

cities are also in this region. The largest is Managua, the nation's capital.

CENTRAL HIGHLANDS East of Managua lies the area known as the central highlands. This mountainous area is covered with dense rainforest and receives an annual rainfall of between 70 and 100 inches. The region is nearly uninhabitable, but in the mountains is a rich mining district called Nueva Segovia. For many decades, a few people have been willing to live in this humid place in order to mine the silver and gold found here.

These Nicaraguans on the Mosquito Coast sell their farm produce from a makeshift hut.

MOSQUITO COAST Even wetter than the central highlands is the Mosquito Coast, which runs along the eastern third of the country from top to bottom. This region is the wettest area in Central America, with average rainfall ranging from 100 to 250 inches per year. Much of the area's soil is gravel and sandy clay, with the only variation being a treeless, grassy plain called the savanna. Four main groups live here: the Miskito, Rama, and Sumo Indians are native to Nicaragua, and the Garífunas are blacks who originated from Africa. These groups have lived in this swamp-like region for many generations. Many build their houses on stilts to protect themselves from floods and snakes.

Few Nicaraguans travel between the Pacific coast and the Mosquito Coast. Only a few roads link the two sides of the country so travel is mostly by plane and boat.

LAKES AND RIVERS

A network of waterways throughout Nicaragua plays an important role in the country's system of transportation, commerce, and daily life. For example, the best farmland is near the lakes, rivers, and seas. Rivers mark the boundaries between Nicaragua and its neighbors, Honduras and Costa Rica. City dwellers often take advantage of a sunny weekend by driving to one of many resorts on the shores of Lakes Managua and Nicaragua.

The larger of these two lakes is Lake Nicaragua, also called *Gran Lago* ("GRAHN LAH-go"), or Great Lake. It is 45 miles wide and 110 miles long, and has three volcanoes and over 300 islands, most of which are inhabited. Perhaps the most remarkable feature is its unique inhabitants— freshwater sharks. The Tipitapa River connects this lake to Lake Managua, which covers 390 square miles.

The Coco River forms part of the border with Honduras, and the San Juan River forms part of the border with Costa Rica before emptying into

Main road in Tipitapa, a town located near the Tipitapa River.

the Caribbean Sea. Other rivers important to Nicaragua's system of transportation include the Escondido and the Río Grande.

Ever since the 16th century, when Christopher Columbus sailed along the coast of what is now Nicaragua, explorers had hoped to find a passage through the isthmus that would connect the Pacific Ocean on the west and the Atlantic Ocean on the east. While the San Juan River does run nearly from coast to coast, it is not suitable for heavy traffic by freighters and other large vessels.

In the 19th century, Americans and Europeans studied a plan to build a canal to join the two oceans, providing a faster and less expensive route to the west coast of the United States from the east coast. The United States formed a committee to find the best place to build the canal. At first they chose Nicaragua, but the Nicaraguan president wanted to set limits on U.S. access to the proposed canal, so the committee reconsidered and selected Panama as the site for the connecting waterway.

The tranquil lakeside setting of Momotombo Volcano belies the destructive force that lurks within.

VOLCANOES AND EARTHQUAKES

Volcanoes are largely responsible for the geographic makeup of Nicaragua. Many lakes and islands were formed by volcanic activity. Cities developed near the volcanoes because fertile farmland there attracted early settlers.

At least a dozen active volcanoes and many more dormant ones give the landscape a beautiful quality, but these peaks also pose a threat to Nicaraguans. About 60% of the population lives near active volcanoes, which means that, at any time, their homes and crops could be destroyed by an eruption or an earthquake caused by underground volcanic activity. This happened to the residents of Managua in 1972. Managua is actually built on top of old volcanic rock that has been pressed together, not on solid rock. More recently, many people in León and nearby towns and villages had to leave their homes in April 1992, when Cerro Negro erupted after 21 years in a dormant state.

Frequent earthquakes have caused destruction to Nicaragua throughout the country's history. The western part of the country lies within the Ring of Fire, a chain of volcanoes and fault lines, or breaks below the ground where earthquakes are likely to happen. It is called the Ring of Fire because the volcanoes are so likely to explode. Other volcanoes in Nicaragua that have erupted in the past two decades include Momotombo,

MOUNTAIN IN MOTION

The explosion of Cerro Negro on April 10, 1992, threw fire 10,000 feet into the sky. Car-sized boulders and scorching sand rained onto the surrounding villages and countryside. A cloud of ash darkened the sky above León and blanketed the city with several inches of dark gray powder.

The volcano, 15 miles southwest of León and 35 miles northwest of Managua, had erupted unexpectedly after lying dormant for 21 years. The blast injured at least 40 people and left two others dead. Sand and ash spewed from the volcano for almost two days, and nearby villages had to be evacuated. After this, the cinder cone was quiet for 28 hours and villagers thought the worst was over. But the 2,378-foot volcano erupted again four days later, releasing about 74 million tons of ash and other material over the course of a few days. Food, homes, and livestock were destroyed and the damage stretched beyond the villages to León, leaving about 23,000 people homeless. It was the 16th time that the volcano had been active since it first erupted in 1867.

San Cristóbal, Telica, and Concepción. Concepción and Madera make up Ometepe Island in Lake Nicaragua, on which at least eight small villages are built—proof that Nicaraguans have learned to coexist with the volcanoes that dominate the skyline.

Although living in the Ring of Fire can be dangerous, the turbulent government and economy of Nicaragua have made it difficult for the country to support research on volcanoes and earthquakes. In 1974, the United States donated seismic equipment to encourage the study of earthquakes and volcanoes, but no one maintained it and it soon became useless. Now, seismologists and volcanologists have set up stations in villages and cities located near volcanoes, where people and equipment monitor the condition of the earth. The Nicaraguan Institute of Territorial Studies is also studying the volcanoes and their effects on the country.

Scientists are discovering ways to use the heat given off by volcanoes to generate energy. They are planning to build a geothermal plant near Cerro Negro, about 10 miles from León. A similar plant exists about 50 miles from Managua, near Momotombo Volcano. The Momotombo Geothermal Plant converts heat generated by the volcano into electricity for Managua and other nearby towns. The plant at Cerro Negro is only in the planning stages, but when completed, it will have twice the capacity of the existing plant at Momotombo.

Near Masaya, the active volcano Santiago billows smoke almost constantly. Rumors have it that during his reign, the dictator Anastasio Somoza García ordered the National Guard to drop political prisoners into Santiago's crater from a helicopter.

CLIMATE AND SEASONS

Managua, the capital, is located about 87 degrees west of the prime meridian, at about the same longitude as Memphis, Tennessee, but it is much closer to the equator than any part of the United States. It lies about 12 degrees north of the equator, or about 750 miles south of Miami. This means that Nicaragua has a tropical climate—warm in the morning, hot and humid in the afternoon, and pleasant at night. In the mountainous regions of northwest Nicaragua, the altitude makes the average temperature a little cooler, especially at night. Also, the northern part of the country is a little less humid than the southern part. Even so, the weather in Nicaragua is hotter and more humid than what most North Americans are used to.

The climate in the eastern part of Nicaragua is always about the same—hot and wet. Few people live there because much of the land is covered with rainforest and jungle. It is the perfect home for monkeys, alligators, and snakes. Bananas, coconuts, persimmons, and other tropical fruits also thrive in this climate.

In the more densely pop- ulated western lowlands, there

Snakes and monkeys thrive in the rainforests, where it is warm and humid.

are two seasons: the wet season from May to November and the dry season from December to April. It is hotter during the dry season. During the wet season, it rains heavily almost every day, and there is little warning before a storm. The sun may be shining in the morning, and then suddenly it is pouring. For a few weeks in July and August, the rain stops altogether and the weather gets very hot. The average temperature in the lowlands is about 86° Fahrenheit. The sun is blazing hot, and Nicaraguans often try to protect themselves from its damaging effects. Women sometimes carry umbrellas to provide some shade if they are out in the open for a long time. Men wear straw hats that tie under the chin to shade their eyes while working in the fields or walking outdoors.

Very few homes have air conditioning—in fact, most do not even have electric fans. In Managua, a few upper-class homes, offices, restaurants, and discotheques have air conditioning, but most people just have to tolerate the heat. Despite the climate, young Nicaraguans faithfully follow fashion fads—even when it means wearing *plásticos* ("plast-EE-koh"), or clothes made of plastic, a style that was popular in the discos in the mid-1980s.

Rich vegetation typical of the country's rainforests.

Government complex in Managua, the capital city beside Lake Managua.

MAJOR CITIES

MANAGUA With a population of about 1.3 million people, Managua is the largest city in Nicaragua. Nearly a third of the population lives here. From the top of Loma de Tiscapa (Tiscapa Hill), the whole city is visible. The most beautiful part of this view is the Tiscapa Lagoon, a shallow lake that shimmers in the sun. The lagoon, which filled in a hole once made by a big volcano, is surrounded by lush green trees.

Managua became an important city in 1852 when two rival political factions settled their differences by choosing the sleepy town as the nation's capital. Before this decision, León and Granada were the two most important cities in Nicaragua. The Liberals dominated León and the Conservatives controlled Granada, and the two groups fought many battles before agreeing to make Managua the capital.

The city has a drawback: since it is situated on a major fault line near a volcano, earthquakes occur frequently. In 1972, a very strong earthquake shook the area. Ten thousand people were killed and the city was destroyed. Recovery has since been a long, slow process that may never be complete. By 1980, about 40% of Managua still lay in ruins and subsequent earthquakes have hindered plans to rebuild it. As a result, Managua has many vacant buildings and poorly constructed makeshift homes in shantytowns.

Over the past two years, however, there have been signs that commerce is picking up. A shopping mall, a Benetton outlet, and billboards advertising Rayban sunglasses have all come to Managua.

GRANADA Nicaragua's oldest city, Granada, was founded in 1524 by the Spanish explorer Francisco Fernández de Córdoba. Like Managua, it is also located on the shore of a lake and near a volcano. It is the country's second largest city and an important commercial area. Granada's volcano has left the area around the town fertile, and coffee and sugarcane are two important products grown there.

This building in Granada reflects the architectural style of the Spanish, who ruled from the 16th to early 19th centuries.

Like all cities in Nicaragua, Granada has seen its share of fighting caused by the political conflict that has ravaged the country for years. Many factories and buildings suffered heavy damage and are still being repaired. There are a hundred or so tiny islands east of Granada in Lake Nicaragua. These *isletas* ("ees-LEH-tahs") are said to have been created when Granada's volcano erupted, blowing its lake-facing side into the water. The islands are linked by motorboat taxis, and rich Nicaraguans have built cottages there for weekend retreats.

LEÓN A smaller city than Managua or Granada, León was also founded by Fernández de Córdoba. In the Spanish colonial period, it was the capital of Nicaragua. León has a huge cathedral built as a result of a mix-up in blueprints. The ruling Spanish government mistakenly sent to León the design for a cathedral in Lima, the capital of Peru, then another Spanish colony. The blueprint for León's cathedral was, in turn, sent to Lima, which explains why that large city has such a tiny cathedral. Outside the city are beaches, resort towns, and a fertile agricultural area. Much of the dry, flat plain around the city is planted with cotton.

NATURAL RESOURCES

Agriculture is a very important part of life in Nicaragua. Almost half of the employed people work on farms. During the dry season, when crops are harvested, schools are closed so that children can help with the farm work.

A variety of food—from beans and bananas to sugarcane and rice—grow well in Nicaraguan soil. Corn, coffee, cotton, tobacco, and cacao are the most important crops. The country's chief exports are coffee, cotton, and sugar. The main imports are cars, machines, and chemicals—things that cannot be produced in Nicaragua because the necessary materials are scarce. Lumber and fish, however, are plentiful natural resources, and the export of these important products contributes to the country's trade revenue. Valuable wood from mahogany, ebony, and rosewood trees that grow in the highland areas is exported to other countries, including the United States, where it is often made into furniture.

About 9%, or 4,500 square miles, of the land is considered arable, or suitable for growing things. Of this land, roughly 1.2 million acres, or 1,875 square miles, are actively cultivated. About 65% of those acres, or 1,218 square miles, is planted with rice and cotton. Another large portion of the land is used for grazing animals that produce dairy products and meat.

SHARK!

Lake Nicaragua is the only freshwater lake in the world that is home to sharks. Stories of missing swimmers abound, but while people suspect the predatory inhabitants, no deaths due to shark attacks have been documented.

The lake was probably formed long ago when volcanic activity cut it off from the Pacific Ocean. For many years, it was believed that this process trapped marine life in the lake while it still contained salt water. As the character of the lake gradually changed to fresh water, the saltwater fish adapted to living in fresh water and were able to reproduce. Another explanation is that the sharks travel back and forth between the Atlantic Ocean and the lake. In 1966, after a decade of research that involved putting identification tags on sharks, American zoologist Thomas B. Thorson reported that bull sharks, a ferocious and versatile predatory species, enter the lake via San Juan River from the Atlantic Ocean, looking for food. The sharks, which can grow to 10 feet and weigh up to 400 pounds, can adapt to fresh water.

Another typically saltwater species found in the lake is the sawfish, which can weigh up to 1,000 pounds. One fisherman caught a large sawfish in 1991, but incidents of catching sharks or sawfish happen rarely today. In the 1950s and 1960s, when the lake's population of these fish was much bigger, commercial fishermen netted thousands of sharks and sawfish. Enrique Sandino, the manager of a fish processing plant in the 1970s, sold shark steaks for nine cents a pound.

FLORA AND FAUNA

Many varieties of plants and animals are indigenous to Nicaragua and other Central American countries. Some of the plants and trees, like cedar, oak, and pine, are just as easily found in Nicaragua as in western Europe or the United States. But because the country's climate varies from region to region, you can also see tropical plants like tamarind and persimmon trees.

Many animal species found in North America also live in some regions of Nicaragua. For example, deer, rattlesnakes, and coyotes are common in the highlands and in some parts of the western lowlands. But because the climate in Nicaragua is different than that in North America, animals usually only seen in zoos in North America inhabit areas of this tropical country, especially the jungles. These exotic animals include toucans, pelicans, sloths, monkeys, jaguars, wild boars, alligators, and snakes.

HISTORY

THE HISTORY OF NICARAGUA goes back to the late Stone Age. Nicaragua has been an independent republic for less than 200 years, and the most important developments in its culture have occurred only over the past century.

The Nicaraguans have been ruled by the Spanish empire, a coalition of Central American states, the U.S. Marines, several dictators, a socialist regime, and now, a democratically elected president and National Assembly. The nation survived nearly 30 years of relative anarchy, followed by several decades of dictatorship and two civil wars.

THE FIRST PEOPLE

Long before Spanish explorers came to Central America in the 16th century, Indian tribes inhabited the area. Anthropologists and archeologists have found evidence that people lived in Nicaragua for about 6,500 years before European explorers "discovered" the new land.

Sometime between 300 B.C. and A.D. 300, the Indians developed simple villages; before that they were cave dwellers. Typically, they were farmers whose main crop was corn. By A.D. 800, the Indian tribes produced intricate works of art, especially pottery. Religion and trading networks became important parts of their lives, and their culture became stratified, which means that some people assumed positions of authority over others.

One of the largest of these tribes was the Nicarao, who inhabited much of the Pacific lowlands. They grew corn (their principal food source),

Above: **A Spanish galleon. In the 16th century, Spanish explorers sailed to the "New World" in ships like these.**

Opposite: **An old tank displayed by the road bears silent testimony to the many battles that have ravaged the country.**

Central plaza in Granada with fountain and bandstand.

sweet potatoes, and cacao beans. Besides eating corn off the ear, they ground it to make *tortillas* ("tohr-TEE-yah").

After Christopher Columbus traveled to Central America and reported to the king of Spain that great wealth could be found there, many Spanish explorers set out for the "New World" in search of riches. As they traveled, they established settlements throughout the region. One of the earlier colonies was in Panama, where Pedro Arias de Avila, or Pedradrias, became the ruler. He sent his lieutenant, Francisco Fernández de Córdoba, on a special mission to nearby Nicaragua, and in 1523, Fernández de Córdoba became the first *conquistador* ("kohn-KEYS-tah-door"), or conqueror, to arrive in Nicaragua.

He founded two cities, Granada and León, and went against Pedrarias's wishes by trying to make Nicaragua a separate Spanish province. By Pedrarias's order, Fernández de Córdoba was beheaded, and Pedrarias became Nicaragua's governor from 1526 to 1531. He conquered the Nicaraguan natives just as he had conquered the Indians in Panama—by force. In fact, the Spaniards conquered large areas of Latin America, forcing its peoples to obey Spanish rules and customs, teaching them the Spanish version of world history, and replacing their religions with the Roman Catholic faith.

Between 1519 and 1650, about two-thirds of all Indians living in Central America lost their lives to the Spaniards through warfare, disease, and slavery. The Nicarao Indians who survived were forced off their land because the *conquistadores* wanted to build cities there. The tribe's cultural identity suffered when the Spanish took over, but one aspect of it still remains today: the word "Nicaragua" comes from the tribe's name and is thought to mean "here near the lake," referring to Lake Nicaragua.

GOVERNING THE COLONIES

As the Spanish empire grew, the king of Spain established a branch of the Spanish government, called the Supreme Council of the Indies, responsible for the colonies in Latin America. The highest office was that of viceroy, which Christopher Columbus (right) held in the early days. Other offices controlled every aspect of life in the colonies, from trade to religion and customs.

Central America was divided into three judicial areas called *audiencias* ("aw-dee-EN-see-ahs"). After 1570, Nicaragua came under the authority of the *audiencia* of Guatemala. The chief executive in each *audiencia* was called the governor, but he served the roles of president, governor, and head of military. The king of Spain appointed the governors. The governor appointed *corregidors* ("koh-reh-GUH-doors"), who ruled smaller towns inhabited mostly by Indians.

SPANISH RULE

The leaders chosen to govern Nicaragua were often cruel to the Indians. Indians had to work on other people's land rather than continue their tradition of farming their own. Being forced to give up traditions like this made the Indians resentful of the government. *Mestizos* ("meh-STEEZ-ohs"), or people of mixed Indian and Spanish descent, tried to avoid forced labor by adopting Spanish customs and denouncing their Indian heritage.

In the 1760s, a new governing structure was introduced. Property owners in each city selected the members of a town council. After the system of local government took root, the position of council member was passed down from father to son. The councilmen appointed local judges. Usually these offices were held by people of Spanish ancestry who were born in and lived in the colonies. As these people rose to prominent positions in Nicaragua, they grew used to running the government without much interference from Spain.

When Charles III became king of Spain in 1759, he tightened the reins on colonial administrations. All over Central America people began thinking about how they could break away from Spain's authority. In 1821, Nicaragua and the rest of Central America declared their independence.

Until the end of the 18th century, Spanish people in Central America lived pretty much as they pleased, however, the Indians were treated rather poorly.

Single-cropping—such as in the picture above —was not prevalent in newly independent Nicaragua, since farmers grew what they needed to consume and only sufficient beyond that for cash to buy what they could not grow or make.

AN INDEPENDENT REPUBLIC

After Nicaragua declared its independence from Spain in 1821, it became part of the Mexican empire. A year later, Nicaragua left the empire to join the United Provinces of Central America, an organization of former Spanish colonies ruled by a central government in Guatemala City. Problems arose when Nicaraguan officials disagreed with the central government about building a canal through Nicaragua. Nicaraguans saw the proposed canal as a way to increase the country's economic activity, but the central government decided it would take business away from ports in Guatemala. Eventually, Nicaraguan officials decided the central government was too far away to understand their needs. In 1838, Nicaragua left the United Provinces and became an independent republic.

Now, each city and village governed itself. In many ways, this system benefited the people living in rural communities because there were no laws restricting their use of the land. Farmers who grew enough food to feed their families were satisfied with their lifestyle of subsistence farming. They had no desire to produce enough goods to export to other nations.

Most of the local leaders, however, agreed that a national government was needed. The patriarchy (educated leaders of local governments who wanted to create a national government) had a vision of Nicaragua as an international power capable of participating in world trade. They embraced new capitalist values and felt that progress meant earning money by trading with other countries.

The first step toward realizing this vision was the creation of a national government to regulate the ownership of land and use of natural resources. The patriarchy needed the cooperation of farmers, but these people were not interested in creating a national government.

At the same time, a difference of political ideas divided the patriarchy itself. Two groups formed that had conflicting ideas of how the country should be run. In many ways, the two groups had similar goals, but they each had a different plan of how to achieve those goals. One group was based in León and became known as the liberal party. The other group, the conservative party, governed Granada. The liberals favored political liberty, while the conservatives favored political order and the ideas of the colonial past. This led to constant warfare between the two groups.

William Walker was an American president of Nicaragua in 1856.

THE TURNING POINT

Finally, something happened that made all of Nicaragua join together to save the country. An American adventurer, William Walker, went to Nicaragua at the request of government officials in León. He was supposed to help them defeat Granada in a battle over which party would control the country. But after a bloody battle, Walker made himself president in 1856. For a year, he ruled the country as an oppressive tyrant. Despite opposition from local leaders, he sold or gave land to American companies, declared English the official language, and legalized slavery. He also tried to make Nicaragua part of the United States.

The actions of José Santos Zelaya, who became president in 1893, set off a chain of events that led to the United States' posting of its Marines in Nicaragua.

The two warring parties of patriarchs joined forces and recruited many peasants to help fight Walker. The people of Nicaragua succeeded in overthrowing Walker and forced him to leave the country.

Once the patriarchs had stopped fighting among themselves, they were able to form a centralized government. From 1857 to 1893, almost all the presidents were conservatives. They passed laws that made it harder for peasants to own land, essentially taking away the farmers' livelihood.

At the beginning of the 19th century, land was wealth, and most Nicaraguans owned at least some land. By 1900, though, distinct class boundaries had formed, dividing poor peasant farmers from the wealthy landowners for whom they worked.

UNITED STATES INVOLVEMENT

Around this time, the matter of building a canal to connect the two oceans once again became a relevant issue, leading to the start of uneasy relations with the United States. José Santos Zelaya, the liberal president who took office in 1893, refused to grant the United States unrestricted rights to build the canal. Many Nicaraguans—especially conservatives—opposed Zelaya, a harsh dictator.

The United States encouraged the conservative opposition to revolt against Zelaya. When two U.S. citizens who participated in the revolt were executed by Zelaya's officers, the United States decided it was time to take direct action. U.S. Marines were sent in to preserve order. Stationed in Bluefields on the Mosquito Coast, the Marines tried to block a liberal victory. When Zelaya resigned in 1909, another liberal, José Madriz, took his place. The U.S. also refused to recognize Madriz. The civil war in Nicaragua continued for several more months until conservative president Adolfo Díaz took office in 1911.

A brief period of relative calm followed. But then Díaz made an agreement that turned over control of the country's finances to the United States as a condition for a loan from U.S. banks. The contract put the United States in charge of Nicaragua's finances until 1925, when the debt would be paid off.

Soon, the Marines were back, this time to deal with the forces that opposed American control. In 1916, a treaty was ratified that gave the United States exclusive rights to build a canal and to establish naval bases. Although the United States later decided to build the canal in Panama instead, it did set up naval bases in several areas of Nicaragua. The Marines occupied Nicaragua almost constantly until 1933, keeping an eye on the government and the opposition.

Eventually, the opposition rallied together under General Augusto César Sandino, who led the rebels from 1927 to 1933. These rebels named themselves Sandinistas after their leader and adopted "guerrilla" tactics, with small groups hiding in the mountains and coming out unexpectedly to attack the Marines.

General Augusto César Sandino. Sandinistas got their name from Sandino.

27

President Anastasio Somoza García, head of the National Guard and the first of the ruling Somozas.

The Sandinistas knew they were greatly outnumbered by the Marines, but they fought anyway. General Sandino's motto was "Free homeland or death," and he often said, "It's better to die a rebel than to live as a slave."

Finally, the United States decided to compromise. Instead of trying to impose democracy, it agreed to support any Nicaraguan leader who could promise peace in Nicaragua and friendship with the United States. In the 1932 election—the last supervised by the United States—a former rebel named Juan Bautista Sacasa became president.

After the election, the Marines left and Nicaragua was on its own. Before they left, however, they trained a new Nicaraguan army to help the president keep order. The handpicked head of this National Guard was a former used-car dealer and health inspector, Anastasio Somoza García.

After the Marines left Nicaragua, President Sacasa and General Sandino signed a peace treaty to end the fighting. But in 1934, General Somoza went behind the president's back and ordered the National Guard to kill Sandino. The Guard also murdered 300 Sandinistas. When President Sacasa tried to take away General Somoza's control over the National Guard, he discovered that General Somoza was much too powerful. In 1936, General Somoza forced President Sacasa (who was his wife's uncle) to resign, and by the following year, the general was president of Nicaragua.

THE SOMOZA DYNASTY

For the next 42 years (1937–1979), the Somoza family ruled the country. President Somoza—called Tacho by his friends and family—was eager to cooperate with the United States and had its support because he was not a Communist and was powerful enough to prevent rebels from causing more war. Under his rule, the Nicaraguan government became stable enough for American corporations to start investing money in business prospects there. The economy expanded, but average Nicaraguans did not see the effects of this improvement.

Somoza had absolute power over the country's activities and used it to his personal advantage. By the 1950s, the Somoza family held much of the country's wealth, while most of the population lived in poverty. When people tried to interfere with Somoza's authority, he had the National Guard threaten or kill them. Because he was completely in charge, Somoza could reelect himself when his first term as president ended in 1941. In 1947, he appointed a family friend to the presidency. In 1950, Somoza again assumed the presidency, but in 1956, at a ball in his honor, a poet, Rigoberto López Pérez, shot him dead in an attempt to end the dictatorship.

Somoza's oldest son Luis took over. During his five years in office, he tried to change the way the country was run. Shortly before he died of a heart attack in 1963, he turned over the presidency to another Somoza family member, who ruled until his own death in 1967.

Luis's younger brother, Anastasio Somoza Debayle, took over the country and ruled by his father's methods. Within a few years as president and head of the National Guard, he had increased his family's wealth to about $900 million. The Somozas owned one-fifth of the country's land, three of its six sugar mills, over 160 factories, an airline, a radio and television station, and several banks.

Anastasio Somoza Debayle, nicknamed Tachito, objected to being called a dictator. Dictators, he argued, do not allow freedom of speech or freedom of the press. He believed that because he allowed Pedro Joaquín Chamorro to publish the newspaper La Prensa, he could not be a dictator. During the Somoza dynasty, however, less than half the population could read. And a newspaper that criticizes the government is not much of a threat to that government as long as the majority of the governed cannot read.

CIVIL WAR AND REVOLUTION

By this time, a distinct upper class had developed that included friends and supporters of the Somozas, corporate leaders who profited from Somoza's unethical economic regime, and a few successful independent business owners. The rest of the population was mostly poor, and they were becoming more aware of Somoza's corruption. Bands of guerrilla rebels began to form and in the early 1970s, the Sandinista National Liberation Front (FSLN) was

Sandinista guards taking a break by a lake. Most of them are drafted into the army at the age of 17. Because of their extreme youth, people called them *los muchachos* ("los moo-CHAH-chohs"), or "the kids."

founded, taking its name and some of its ideas from the rebels who fought under General Sandino in the 1920s. The FSLN members wanted Somoza out of office. They wanted to form a new government that would teach people to read and write, improve health care, provide food and housing, and give political power to workers and peasants. It was dangerous to be known as a Sandinista because the National Guard imprisoned or killed people whom they believed were associated with the FSLN.

Two events brought Somoza's abuse of power out into the open. First, in 1972 Somoza and his National Guard were accused of taking advantage of the terrible earthquake that destroyed Managua. Humanitarian aid poured in from all over the world, but very little of it actually made it into the hands of the people. Supplies, food, blankets, and medicines were allegedly confiscated by Somoza and his officers and sold to poor people living in tent cities.

In addition, Somoza used the tragedy to increase his personal wealth. He saw that homes would need to be rebuilt and the roads would need repaving, so he went into business manufacturing building materials and paving stones. He knew that people would have to take buses to travel to and from their temporary homes outside Managua, so he bought a bus company and gained all the profits. Many people believe that Somoza even put some of the foreign donations right into his own bank account. (Somoza wrote a book called *Nicaragua Betrayed,* in which he explained his side of the story. He denied all the accusations of corruption following the earthquake.)

As more people found out about Somoza's abuse of power, the FSLN gained popularity. When the second event—the assassination of newspaper editor Pedro Joaquín Chamorro—occurred in 1978, the public was outraged. Nicaraguans loved Chamorro because he stood up to Somoza and printed articles in his newspaper, *La Prensa,* describing Somoza's corruption. Many people believed that Somoza had ordered Chamorro's murder. Over 50,000 demonstrators, many of them members of the FSLN, showed up at Chamorro's funeral. Conflicts that broke out between the FSLN and the National Guard led to a civil war. In July 1979, Somoza announced his resignation and fled the country.

NEW REBELS—THE CONTRA WAR

The Sandinistas ruled Nicaragua from 1979 to 1990. They tried to help the poor and improve the economy, but after a brief period of improvement, a new civil war began to take its toll on the economy and hamper the Sandinistas' efforts at social reform.

By the early 1980s, a new group of rebels had formed. They were called counter-revolutionaries (or contras) because they had grown disillusioned with the revolution and opposed the changes the Sandinistas were trying to make. Some contras were former National Guard members who set up military bases in neighboring Costa Rica and Honduras, from where they conducted armed raids into Nicaraguan territory.

In 1981, the United States accused the Nicaraguan government of supplying weapons to rebels in other Central American countries, but in reality, it was the contras who were training with Honduran soldiers. The U.S. government also believed that the Sandinistas were Communists who would allow Russia to set up military bases in Nicaragua. Although the Sandinistas had no intention of allowing Russian military bases, they did

TIMELINE

1500s to 1821	—	Spanish rule.
1838	—	Nicaragua becomes an independent republic.
1820s to 1850s	—	Constant warfare between Granada and León.
1856	—	William Walker appoints himself president.
1890s to 1933	—	U.S. Marines occupy Nicaragua for most of this period.
1934	—	General Augusto César Sandino and 300 of his followers are killed by the National Guard.
1937	—	Somoza regime begins.
1956	—	Anastasio Somoza García is shot and killed by a poet.
1967	—	Anastasio Somoza Debayle takes office.
1978	—	Pedro Joaquín Chamorro is murdered by the National Guard.
1979	—	Sandinistas overthrow Somoza.
1980s	—	Contra war against Sandinista regime.
1990	—	Violeta de Barrios Chamorro wins presidential election.

accept money and military aid from Russia and Cuba, another Communist country. Since United States officials perceived this as a threat to American freedom and democracy, U.S. President Ronald Reagan authorized military aid to the contras and declared a trade embargo on Nicaragua.

Amid escalating tensions, the Sandinistas gladly accepted military aid from Russia in the form of tanks, fighter aircraft, and helicopter gunships. The United States, on its part, commenced almost continuous large-scale joint maneuvers with Honduran troops near the Honduras-Nicaragua border.

The contra war lasted until 1990 when a new president was elected. The winning campaign of Violeta de Barrios Chamorro, the first female president, was endorsed by the United States because she planned to establish democracy in Nicaragua and introduce a free market economy.

GOVERNMENT

NICARAGUA HAS SURVIVED dictatorships and a socialist-style government, and is now trying to create a democracy. Historically, transitions from one government to the next have never been peaceful in Nicaragua, but Violeta Chamorro's victory over former president Daniel Ortega initially appeared to mark the first time one political party had peacefully transferred power to another. The peace, however, did not last long. Two rebel groups are still trying to gain control of the country, and frequent armed conflicts between them are making it hard for the government to concentrate on governing.

Above: **A government-organized May Day rally in Managua, in which workers celebrate the progress made since the country's independence.**

Opposite: **Daniel Ortega became president when the Sandinistas came into power.**

THE RIGHTS OF THE PEOPLE

When Nicaragua belonged to the United Provinces of Central America, its people lived under the region's constitution, approved in 1824. Then in 1826, Nicaragua drew up its own state constitution, and in 1838 it became a nation and drew up a new constitution to reflect this change. All of these constitutions were written by liberals, so they guarded against tyranny and protected the freedom of the people.

Each branch of government had defined areas of responsibility so no one branch had too much power. The conservatives thought these constitutions limited the powers of the executive branch of the government too much. They also felt that the constitutions should only allow for private ownership of land, not collective ownership. Between 1838 and 1974, Nicaragua had 10 different constitutions. The latest, adopted in 1987, guards against absolute governmental power; protects freedom of speech, the press, and religion; and guarantees the right to own land.

KEY POLITICAL PLAYERS

FSLN The *Frente Sandinista Liberación Nacional* ("FREN-tay san-din-EES-tah li-verhr-AH-see-yahn nah-see-yah-NAHL"— Sandinista National Liberation Front) began as a small group of students who opposed Somoza's oppressive rule. The leader, Carlos Fonseca (left), urged the group to take up arms and revolt against the government. Soon, the FSLN became an underground movement that involved many young people who were willing to risk their lives to free their country from Somoza's grip.

Taking inspiration from Fidel Castro's revolution in Cuba, the FSLN assigned bands of guerrilla fighters to live in the mountains and carry out surprise attacks on Somoza's National Guard. After nearly falling apart several times, it finally developed into a revolutionary army capable of overthrowing Somoza. When the group succeeded, it selected people from within its ranks, together with other anti-Somoza organizations, to form a ruling junta (political faction). In 1984, the Sandinista party won the presidential election.

CONTRAS They are the rebels who opposed the revolutionary government (the Sandinistas). They include Somocistas, people who had profited from Somoza's abuse of power and feared revenge by the new government. When the Somoza regime fell, many Somocistas fled the country even though the Sandinistas outlawed the death penalty and pardoned many of Somoza's collaborators.

Many business and political leaders were glad to see Somoza overthrown but did not fully agree with the Sandinistas' idea to redistribute the country's wealth. Some of them joined the FSLN to try to influence its policies, but when they realized the Sandinistas intended to carry out their original plans, they resigned from their government positions and helped to organize the contras. One of these people was Violeta Chamorro, the only female member of the original five-member ruling junta selected by the Sandinistas. She left her position in the junta only nine months after being appointed to it. The largest contra group was the Nicaraguan Democratic Force (FDN). Of its 48 commanders, 46 were former members of Somoza's National Guard. Their bases were mostly along the northern part of Nicaragua's border with Honduras. The other anti-Sandinista groups in the south did not join the FDN at first because of its link to the National Guard.

UNO The *Unión Nacional Oposicion* ("YOO-nee-yahn nah-see-yah-NAHL ah-po-ZIH-see-yahn"—National Opposition Union) is a 14-party coalition of anti-Sandinista organizations. It backed Chamorro in the 1990 election, but the coalition suffered from internal divisions. In 1993, after accusations of corruption within the government, the UNO severed its ties with Chamorro and boycotted the National Assembly, leaving the Sandinistas in the majority.

UNITED STATES The United States feared that the Sandinistas were Communists and would allow Russia to set up military bases in Nicaragua. The U.S. government opposed the Sandinistas and aided the contras to protect U.S. interests. President Ronald Reagan (above) sent the contras weapons, money, and soldiers.

In 1984, he charged the Sandinistas with setting up a Communist dictatorship and in 1985, imposed a trade embargo against Nicaragua after Congress voted against his $14 million contra-aid plan. Before the trade embargo, the United States was Nicaragua's chief trading partner. A year later, the Reagan administration was accused of diverting profits from secret arms sales to Iran to the contras, even after Congress had prohibited any more military aid to the rebels. Further investigation into the Iran-contra scandal concluded with an official report that members of Reagan's administration had acted illegally.

The U.S. Central Intelligence Agency (C.I.A.) also helped the contras. The C.I.A. participated in the bombing of Managua Airport and helped blow up oil pipelines in several ports. It also directed an operation to place explosive mines in the harbor at the port of Corinto, preventing ships carrying supplies from reaching land. In 1986, the World Court, the judicial arm of the United Nations, ruled that the United States was at fault for "training, arming, equipping, financing, and supplying the contra forces." But the World Court has no authority to enforce its decisions.

Sandinista revolutionary statue in Managua.

THE SANDINISTAS' SOCIALIST REGIME

SOCIALISM In a socialist regime, the national government is made up of a multimember directorate, but there is no concrete system of checks and balances. Typically, the government has complete control over the country's economy. The military plays a very important role because it enforces the policies made by the governing body. A simplified explanation of traditional socialism focuses on equality. Socialists object to personal ownership of property because they believe that a country's wealth should be equally earned and shared by everyone.

The Sandinista ideology follows socialism to some extent, but the Sandinistas always asserted that their revolutionary plan was specifically tailored to Nicaraguan needs. They wanted to bring about equality and national prosperity, and hoped to narrow the enormous gap between the rich and poor. They confiscated property owned by wealthy Somoza supporters and turned it into state-run farming collectives, but two out of three farms remained privately owned.

WHO IS IN CHARGE? From 1979 to 1984, the ruling body of the Sandinista government was a five-person junta selected from the FSLN and other groups that opposed Somoza. One of its members was Violeta Chamorro. During the first year, however, Chamorro and another member disagreed with the Sandinistas' new policies, so they left the government and formed opposition parties. Then, in a free election, Daniel Ortega was elected president of the Sandinista government. Some

WHERE THE SANDINISTAS FAILED

The Sandinistas wanted to unite the historically isolated eastern coast with the rest of the country, but in their attempts, they made mistakes. Many Miskito Indians there opposed unification because they thought it would jeopardize their control over the area's natural resources. The Sandinista government suspected Miskitos of being contras, and there were cases where they killed or imprisoned them. The contras had been known to kidnap Indians and take them to military bases and refugee camps in Honduras, where some were forced to join the contra army. Trying to reduce the possibility of contra influence on the Indians, the Sandinistas uprooted entire Indian communities from areas near the fighting and moved them to "safer" places.

The Sandinista government also had the habit of unfairly arresting and jailing people it believed to be supporting the contras, including politicians and union leaders. Critics of the government cited its violation of religious freedom and the right to free speech. For example, executive orders repeatedly shut down the newspaper *La Prensa* because it published anti-government opinions. Also, in 1985, the government forced 10 foreign priests to leave Nicaragua because they gave anti-government sermons. The military draft was another highly criticized Sandinista action.

political groups say that the 1984 election was one of the fairest in Central American history, but others said it was unfair because opposition parties were not given enough freedom to campaign, so they had no real chance of winning. In addition to the president and the National Assembly, the Sandinistas established a Council of State, a coalition of representatives from various political parties, labor unions, and business associations. The council acted as an advisory board to the lawmakers.

POLICIES, GOALS, AND IDEALS In their first few years in power, the Sandinistas' main goals were to raise the standard of living and to make everyone more equal by redistributing the country's wealth. For the past four decades, most of the land, industries, and money had belonged to the Somozas and their friends. Immediately after taking office, the Sandinistas began giving the land to peasants so that they could grow enough food for their families. The next step was the nationalization of private industries. The economy took a slight upward turn when the Sandinistas began controlling agricultural exports, banking and finance, insurance, and mining. Businesses and farms owned by private citizens not affiliated with Somoza were allowed to continue normal operations.

The assassination of newspaper editor Pedro Joaquín Chamorro gave rise to much public outrage, which eventually led to the downfall of the Somoza regime.

RETURN TO DEMOCRACY— PRESIDENT CHAMORRO

In a democratic election supervised by neutral organizations, Violeta Chamorro defeated incumbent Daniel Ortega and several other candidates. Before she decided to run for president, she was best known as the widow of Pedro Joaquín Chamorro, the editor of an antigovernment newspaper who was assassinated during Somoza's regime. The U.S. government endorsed her campaign because she planned to establish a democratic society and a free-market economy.

THE STRUCTURE OF DEMOCRACY The national government consists of three branches: the executive, legislative, and judicial. In Nicaragua, the people vote directly to elect the president for a six-year term, and anyone over 16 can vote. The president appoints ministers to head different ministries.

Nicaragua is divided into 16 departments (much like provinces). Based on its population, each department gets a certain number of representatives in the National Assembly, the legislative branch of the government. There is a total of 90 elected representatives in the National Assembly, which is similar to the U.S. Congress.

The judicial branch consists of several court districts spread out over the country, each district representing several departments. The Supreme Court is in Managua, and the next highest courts are five "Chambers of Second Instance," located in León, Granada, Masaya, Matagalpa, and Bluefields.

The key players in the Chamorro administration include Chief Minister Antonio Lacayo (the president's son-in-law) and army head General Humberto Ortega Saavedra, former President Ortega's brother. Chamorro retained the general as temporary head of army, even though he had been a ruling Sandinista commander for 10 years, to ensure the Sandinistas would comply with the government's requirement to disarm by June 1990. In return for the favor of keeping one of their men in such a high position, the Sandinistas respected the new government's power to reduce the size of the military and determine how it would be used. The decision angered the contras.

Violeta Chamorro, the first woman president of Nicaragua.

In January 1993, Chamorro added three more Sandinistas to her Cabinet and announced a new economic plan with emphasis on social issues that appealed to the Sandinistas. The plan also meant a 20% devaluation of the córdoba (the Nicaraguan currency) and a freeze on government spending. These actions were part of the reason the UNO ended its support of Chamorro.

POLICIES, GOALS, AND IDEALS The main goal of the new government was to end the fighting between the contras and the Sandinistas. Many of Chamorro's early decisions revolved around procedures for disarmament—getting the soldiers to give up their weapons. Chamorro thought that once this was done, she and her administration could move on to their other primary goal: dismantling the socialist-style institutions erected by the Sandinistas and returning the country to a more Western-style democracy and free market economy.

One of the early goals of Violeta Chamorro's government was to end the fighting between the contras and Sandinistas.

POLITICAL STRUGGLE CONTINUES

Before Chamorro took office, there were frequent battles between the contras and Sandinistas. Both parties were reluctant to lay down arms for fear the other side would attack and they would be defenseless. Just days before Chamorro's inauguration, the outgoing Sandinista government, the contra rebels, and Chamorro's representatives signed agreements to establish an immediate ceasefire. Five security zones were created for the contras to prepare for demobilization without fear of a Sandinista attack—the Sandinistas agreed to stay at least 12 miles away from these zones. The contras agreed to begin surrendering all weapons to international authorities on April 25, 1990, and to complete demobilization by June 10, 1990.

The transition of power began peacefully: Ortega went to Chamorro's home after the election to pledge his cooperation, and the agreements signed a few days before Chamorro took office allowed 22,000 contras and their families to return from Honduras, turn their weapons over to the authorities, and go back to their homes. Not all accepted this offer. Estimates of the still-armed contras varied between 550 and 700 in 1990, but since then many more have taken up arms again. These rebels are called *recontras* ("ray-KOHM-pah"). Former members of the Sandinista army, called *recompas* ("ray-KOHN-trah"), are now fighting against the current government as well as the recontras.

Chamorro had been president only three months when the recompas attacked again. In July 1990, a violent strike led by a Sandinista labor federation paralyzed Managua. The official army, still led by Sandinistas, was sent to restore order, but Chamorro had to make a deal with the rebels. She promised to stop renting state-owned land to private growers and to consult with the Sandinistas before selling state-owned industries.

Outbreaks of violence continue to trouble the nation. In July 1993, a group of about 150 recontra rebels captured the northern city of Estelí. The ensuing battle left 45 people dead. Two months later, recontras took 38 government officials hostage and demanded the dismissal of Chamorro's head of the army (General Humberto Ortega) and her chief of staff (Antonio Lacayo) in exchange for their release. The next day, the recompas took 34 hostages at UNO headquarters in Managua, including Vice-President Virgilio Godoy Reyes. They demanded the release of the other hostages and $17 billion in war reparations from the United States. The situation was resolved within a week when the recontras were promised extra government protection from recompas attacks.

Many of the Chamorro administration's actions have prompted Nicaraguans and outsiders alike to ask, "Who is really ruling Nicaragua?" When Ortega was voted out of office, the Sandinista Party retained enough seats in the National Assembly to prevent constitutional change. Sandinista influence in the government is still very strong, and a January 1993 article in *Time* magazine reported, "UNO officially broke with Chamorro, and marched through the streets of Managua vowing to drive her from power." It is hard to say whether Chamorro—without support from UNO, the recontras, or the recompas—will make much progress in her remaining years as president.

Sandinista memorial to members killed in battle.

43

ECONOMY

NEW BUSINESSES, shops, restaurants, and super-markets have sprung up all over Managua, the capital city, since a free market economy returned to Nicaragua. Gone are the days of state-run farms and government-controlled banks. Nicaragua now sports the look of an up-and-coming commercial enterprise, but looks can be deceiving. Despite President Chamorro's pledge to protect the poor people, Nicaraguans have watched their standard of living go from bad to worse. Jobs are scarce, health care is prohibitively expensive, and the majority cannot afford to feed and clothe their families. A Benetton store opened in 1991, but who has $33 to spend on a T-shirt? For many in Nicaragua, that is more than a week's salary.

Nicaragua's economy is based on agriculture, which accounts for about a third of the country's gross domestic product (GDP, or the amount of money spent on products and services in a country in a given year). Natural resources include fertile soil, a tropical climate, abundant forests, and oceans. The Sandinistas tried to make Nicaragua a self-supporting nation by teaching more people how to grow food and giving them land, seeds, and supplies. Now that the Chamorro administration has returned much of that land to its pre-revolution owners, many of those poor farmers earn their meager livings by selling brooms or shining shoes in parking lots outside the expensive shopping centers.

Above: **Life goes on for the poor.**

Opposite: **For many in Nicaragua, the national lottery (depicted in the wall painting) holds the tantalizing answer to their needs.**

The córdoba oro.

A TROUBLED ECONOMY

In 1988, inflation reached 36,000%. From 1950 to 1977, the average annual economic growth rate was fairly stable, but from 1981 to 1990 the GDP fell an average of 2.4% yearly. Per capita income (the average income) fell by an annual average of 5.6% during the same period, reaching a low of $300 in 1989. These figures reflect the economic problems caused by guerrilla wars, the U.S. trade embargo, changes in the Central American Common Market trade, floods, drought, and changing commodity prices.

When Chamorro took office in 1990, she introduced a new currency. The *córdoba oro* ("KOHR-doh-bah ORH-oh") started off equal to the U.S. dollar, but by May 1993 the exchange rate was five córdobas to the dollar. The nation's GDP is growing by less than 1% yearly, and about 70% of the people still live in poverty.

EMPLOYMENT AND WAGES

While the installation of a free market economy allowed entrepreneurs to start new businesses and revitalize old ones, the majority lacked the training, skill, and organization to take full advantage of the unfamiliar capitalist system. Many workers lost their jobs when Chamorro sold under-productive industries formerly owned by the Sandinista government to wealthy private citizens. In February 1992, unemployment was reported at 40%, and by August it had gone up to 60%.

The government reported in 1991 that about 55% of the population worked in "micro-enterprises;" this is another way of saying they are not officially employed. These people try to make ends meet by entering the "informal sector" of the economy, becoming street vendors who sell food, clothing, newspapers, and anything else they can get their hands on. Others wash cars or do laundry. On a really good day, they make $6–7.

In 1992, the minimum wage for urban workers—$30–45 a month—did not nearly cover the cost of a subsistence diet for a family of six, and many Nicaraguan families have six or more children. The average teacher's salary is only about $34 a month.

AGRICULTURE

Agriculture, Nicaragua's leading economic activity, accounts for about 30% of the GDP. Almost half the country's workforce does some type of agricultural work. The most valuable crops are coffee and cotton. Other important farm products include corn, beans, sugarcane, and bananas. Rice is the main food crop raised for use in Nicaragua, while most of the coffee is exported.

In Nicaragua, land means wealth as agriculture is the leading economic activity.

The Chamorro administration is giving land back to the people who owned it before the revolution. Small farms considered inefficient were the first to be returned or sold. The government also dismantled state farms and cooperatives as it promoted a return to private ownership.

Many peasants worried that the new landowners would not hire them to work on the farms where they had worked for the past ten years. They were also concerned that if hired, they would be treated poorly, as most farm laborers were in the days of the Somoza regime. In addition, farmers have little incentive to produce more because prices for farm products are low. It is also harder for them to get bank credit to buy machinery and other equipment. For these reasons, many people are leaving farms for cities, hoping to find better jobs. But there are few job openings there either.

Managua, the capital, is also the industrial and commercial center.

INDUSTRIES

The production and sale of consumer goods is slowly starting to increase in Nicaragua, as the government is encouraging industries to take advantage of the country's natural resources. The most important manufactured goods are processed food and beverages, textiles, and products made from wood, chemicals, and minerals.

Forestry, a lucrative activity in the 1970s, is again expanding as many sawmills destroyed during the contra war are being rebuilt. The country also has many mineral deposits not exploited because of insufficient financing, and the government is trying to find foreign backers for several mining projects.

The Sandinista government owned about a third of the manufacturing companies in the 1980s; the rest were privately owned—25% of them by foreigners. Today, developing private industries are producing a variety of consumer goods. Many of the raw materials used in manufacturing have to be imported, especially machinery, transport equipment, metals, and petroleum. While it does not produce enough goods to export, Nicaragua has a plentiful supply of shrimps, lobsters, and fish to trade with other countries. The leading service industry is wholesale and retail trade, particularly the marketing of farm products.

COST OF LIVING

During Sandinista rule, many basic necessities were in short supply. For example, in 1988, a pound of rice cost about $4 and a bar of soap, $10. The typical monthly income for a working class family was only about $400, but the cost of enough rice for the family for a month was about $280. That did not leave much for buying other household items or clothes.

Now, the situation is improving, but it is taking a long time. Local production is down after so many years of destructive civil war, and the Chamorro government is not as generous with basic food subsidies or credit purchases as the Sandinistas were. With the U.S. trade embargo lifted, food and household items imported from the United States and other countries are generally available, but people still cannot afford to buy them. In 1992, the minimum wage was between $30 and $45 a month, but the average cost of enough food for one family ranged from $160 to $192 a month.

In the late 1980s, more than half of the national budget was spent on defense. The Chamorro government has cut back greatly on defense spending, which is a huge step forward. But it has also drastically reduced the budget for job-creation programs, health care, education, and public transportation—all essential services, especially for poor and working-class people. If they cannot find jobs, get medicine when they are sick, learn a marketable skill, or get to a job interview, people cannot support themselves.

Most Nicaraguans depend on public transport to get from one place to another, although the buses are often slow and overcrowded.

49

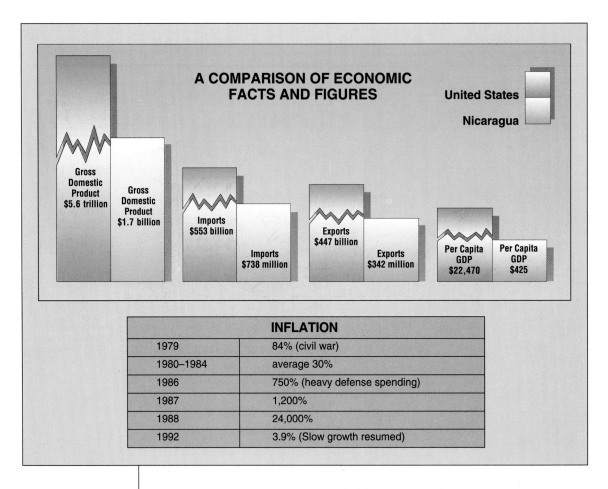

A COMPARISON OF ECONOMIC FACTS AND FIGURES

United States

Nicaragua

Gross Domestic Product $5.6 trillion

Gross Domestic Product $1.7 billion

Imports $553 billion

Imports $738 million

Exports $447 billion

Exports $342 million

Per Capita GDP $22,470

Per Capita GDP $425

INFLATION	
1979	84% (civil war)
1980–1984	average 30%
1986	750% (heavy defense spending)
1987	1,200%
1988	24,000%
1992	3.9% (Slow growth resumed)

FOREIGN AID AND DEBT

When the Sandinistas took over the running of the country in 1979, they inherited an economy in ruins. The Somozas had left the country with a staggering $1.5 billion foreign debt and well-to-do citizens had taken out an additional $1.5 billion to shelter it in U.S. banks, real estate, and other businesses.

During the 1980s, when U.S. President Reagan declared an all-out economic war on the Sandinistas by imposing a trade embargo, Nicaragua's already unstable economy took a further beating.

Now, such trade sanctions have been lifted and Nicaragua is under the rule of the Chamorro government, but the biggest source of foreign

Author Roger Lancaster revealed an interesting difference between Nicaraguan and U.S. workers in his book, *Life is Hard*. A young Nicaraguan man named Elvis asked him, "Why is it that whenever you see a *gringo* ["GREEN-goh," North American] walking, they're always walking fast, like they're in a hurry to get somewhere?"

Lancaster replied, ". . .we are usually in a hurry because—well, we have a saying: 'Time is money.'"

Elvis responded, "I'm for developing the economy, but it would be a tragedy if Nicaragua developed into a society where time is money."

In Rita Golden Gelman's book, *Inside Nicaragua,* she recounts her meeting with a Nicaraguan man who had worked in Miami for a year. He told her: "I earned a lot of money. But I really didn't like it. I felt like a machine. I had to be places at an exact time. Work without talking. Watch the clock for my breaks. That's not how I want to live. It's dehumanizing."

income in Nicaragua still has nothing to do with exported products. Aid from industrial nations totals twice what the country makes from selling its products abroad. In 1989 and 1990, economic aid from other countries averaged $600 million per year. The former Soviet Union is believed to have granted almost half of that amount, and the rest came primarily from the United States, Canada, and the European Community.

In 1991, U.S. aid to Nicaragua totaled $384 million. In 1992, the United States suspended $104 million in aid, about half of which was released at the end of the year. The remainder had not been distributed when President Bill Clinton took office, and his administration had more pressing matters to deal with in 1993. The Nicaraguan government is concerned that its programs to keep the economy stable will fail unless more aid is received, but the threat of more political upheaval scares off foreign investors.

Chamorro is hoping more for donations than loans because its foreign debt is already too big to pay. Reduced foreign exchange earnings in the mid-1980s, partly because of the U.S. trade embargo, made it impossible for the Nicaraguan government to pay off any of its $10.3 billion debt. If Nicaragua's foreign debt was divided equally among its citizens, each Nicaraguan would owe about $2,500.

Nicaragua owes billions of dollars to countries that have provided it with loans, and the government is hoping for outright donations in the future.

NICARAGUANS

NICARAGUANS, or Nicas, as they like to call themselves, are typically friendly and generous people. Despite the war-torn condition of their country, Nicas keep their spirits up and face the nation's economic and political problems with a willingness to make the best of a bad situation. Even in the worst food shortages, anyone who has food will share with someone who is hungry, and Nicas never hesitate to open their homes to visitors. American anthropologists and writers have reported that they were shown the

Above: **Despite Nicaragua's political and economic problems, adults and children alike have resigned themselves to making the best of a bad situation.**

Opposite: **Whether they are of African, Spanish, or Indian descent, the people take pride in their Nicaraguan nationality.**

same hospitality that the locals bestow on each other. And Nicas love to talk. They share stories, talk about their families, and gossip about what goes on around the neighborhood. They generally display a strong pride in their homeland, and their nationality is very important to them.

Nicaraguans have different ethnic origins. The majority of the people are mestizos, people of mixed Spanish and Indian ancestry, but several other ethnic groups make up the rest of the population: Indians, Creoles, black Caribs, and Spaniards. Most of the Indians, Creoles, and blacks live in the eastern part of the country, while the western part is inhabited mainly by mestizos. The geography of the country makes it hard to get from one coast to the other, so people identify more with the region they live in than with the nation as a whole. The distance between the two coasts has resulted in regional loyalties and characteristics.

POPULATION FACTS: A COMPARISON

	Nicaragua	United States
Population	3,878,000	256,561,250
Urban population	60%	76%
Age distribution: 0–14	45.8%	21.7%
15–59	49.9%	61.4%
60 & over	4.3%	16.9%
Population growth	3.1%	0.5%
Population density (people per square mile)	77	70
Life expectancy: men	61	72
women	66	79
Infant mortality (per 1,000 live births)	57	10

ETHNIC GROUPS

Six minority groups live mainly along the Atlantic coast: Miskitos, Ramas, and Sumos are Indians whose ancestors were natives of the land before Spanish colonization; Creoles and black Caribs are of African descent; and Garífunas ("gahr-EE-foo-nahs") have a mix of Indian and African ancestry.

Although the remoteness of the Atlantic coast makes it hard to conduct an accurate census of the area, estimates from the early 1980s place the region's minority, or non-mestizo, population at 36%. Of the estimated 72,600 Indians in the region, over 90% are Miskitos. In the 17th and 18th centuries, the Miskito tribe expanded by conquering other Indian tribes. By 1850, they occupied the entire Mosquito Coast, which extends from Panama in the south to Honduras in the north. Before the 1979 revolution, Miskitos lived mainly in small villages and practiced small-scale farming and fishing. They also participated in some seasonal salaried labor for foreign-owned companies. Today, Miskitos are involved in local government and work in most sectors of the economy.

About 5,000 Sumos live in small isolated communities along the coast

Women are an important part of the workforce.

and in a few larger villages in the Bambana River basin. Many Sumo communities were taken over by Miskitos in the 17th and 18th centuries. An even smaller tribe is the Rama, only about 600 of whom still live in Nicaragua. They live on Rama Cay, a small island in the Bay of Bluefields, and in Monkey Point, a village south of Bluefields. In the 18th century they moved a lot to avoid being captured by Miskitos and sold to the British as slaves.

A modern whitewashed church in Bluefields, where most Creoles and Garífunas live.

Nearly a tenth of the Atlantic coast population has some African ancestry. Black Caribs first came to the area as slaves from British colonies in the West Indies. They remained there after slavery was abolished in 1824 and today live mainly in the Pearl Lagoon area.

Creoles are people of African and Spanish (or other European) descent. In the 17th century, the British brought Africans to the coast to work as slaves on their plantations. When the British lost control of the region, many Africans stayed, either as freed or escaped slaves, or as slaves of the few British who remained in the area. Around the same time, Jamaican merchants began arriving on the coast. In the 19th century, U.S. lumber and banana companies attracted blacks from the southern United States and the Antilles Islands in the West Indies. Today, most Creoles live in Bluefields and the surrounding area. Many are skilled or semi-skilled workers, and some are office employees, technicians, or professionals.

Fishing is a thriving industry along the eastern coast, which overlooks the Caribbean Sea.

Garífunas resemble blacks in physical appearance, but their culture derives from several Latin American Indian groups. Their ancestors lived on the island of St. Vincent until the Carib War in 1795–1797. After the war, the British sent the survivors to an island in the Bay of Honduras. Over half the people died during the trip; only about 2,000 arrived safely. Later, the Garífunas migrated to Nicaragua for better jobs in the mahogany industry and on banana plantations. Most of the 1,500 Garífunas in Nicaragua today live at Pearl Lagoon and Bluefields.

Even on the Atlantic side of Nicaragua, mestizos make up 64% of the population. They are concentrated in the northern department of Zelaya. They began moving east during the second half of the 19th century and founded the small town Rama, which became an important center of commerce.

CULTURAL DIFFERENCES

The two coasts of Nicaragua are like two different countries. People on one side rarely know much about life on the other. The main natural resources of the two areas are quite different, and lifestyles are different. Farmers in the western Pacific lowlands know a lot about corn, cotton, and coffee, while farmers in the east are used to growing coconuts and bananas. The main industries along the Atlantic coast are fishing and catching lobsters. On the Pacific coast there are many more schools, colleges, and businesses. In the east, many Indians follow the traditions and customs of their ancestors. On the whole, the people of western Nicaragua think the Atlantic coast people are rather backward.

A black child of the
Atlantic coast.

Sometimes, cultural differences result in prejudice or racism. Some mestizos on the western coast think blacks from the east are dirty and stupid, and they might move away from a black person on a crowded bus. While most Nicaraguans do not have such prejudices, skin color is a very important trait among mestizos. Lighter skin is associated with beauty and sex appeal, and darker skin is seen as a shortcoming. Nicas typically think that light-skinned people are wealthier than people with darker skin.

Ethnic identity became an important issue only recently. Past governments mostly ignored the Atlantic coast, but when the Sandinistas came to power, they guaranteed civil rights for blacks and Indians and made ethnic identity a political issue. They promoted respect for traditional Indian religions, languages, and celebrations but sometimes offended the Indians by trying to integrate them with the rest of Nicaragua. What the Indians really wanted was independence and control of the abundant natural resources in the region. Peace between the government and the Indians came when the Sandinistas helped organize an autonomous (independent) local government to regulate life on the Atlantic coast.

A black child of the Atlantic coast.

SOCIAL STRUCTURE

Throughout the 20th century, distinct social classes have existed in Nicaraguan culture. During the Somoza dictatorship, a very small upper class owned almost 80% of the land, while the rest of the people were poor, landless, and struggling to feed their families. In the 1970s, over half the people earned only $250 each year. People were very rich or very poor; there was virtually no middle class.

After the revolution, the Sandinistas tried to shrink the gap between the rich and the poor by redistributing land confiscated from large landowners to peasants. Perhaps this idea might have worked eventually, but the contras specifically targeted farms and other food production facilities, destroying the Sandinistas' efforts. Now, President Chamorro is moving the country back toward capitalism, and wealthy upper-class people can get their land back.

Over the last decade or so, a fairly large middle class has emerged, made up of families who have the basic necessities and maybe a few luxuries,

58

such as a refrigerator or relatively new clothes. Usually, these
families must have two incomes
to maintain their lifestyle. Most
Nicaraguans would probably be
considered working-class,
which means they have to work
hard just to make ends meet.
They are not poor, but they earn
only enough money to
buy food and other essentials.
Many other people in the country
still live in poverty.

How much power and op-
portunity people have usually
depends on their job. Farmers

**Nicaraguans lining up
for visas to travel to
the United States.**

usually do not have much political power, and they do not have many
opportunities to advance to a higher social standing. The Sandinistas tried
unsuccessfully to change this fact of Nicaraguan life, but the main factor
that determines what kind of jobs people will have is the family they are
born into. Poor families have been poor for many generations, and they
often feel that there is no way to change their lives.

Unfortunately, this is usually true. It is hard for children of poor farmers
to grow up to be wealthy business owners, for example. Often they do not
finish school in order to help with the farm work. Children born to wealthy
parents, on the other hand, have a much better chance of attending private
schools or finishing their education in foreign countries. In Nicaragua,
wealth equals power, and power brings opportunity.

LEAVING THEIR HOMELAND

Although Nicas possess a strong love of their homeland, the two civil wars that have ravaged the country over the past 15 years have induced many to seek refuge in other countries. Even before the revolution, people were leaving Nicaragua to escape oppression. Since 1979, somewhere between 5% and 15% of the population has left Nicaragua because of conflicts between the government and opposition forces. (Estimates vary greatly because some include only refugees and exiles, whiles others also count the contras and their families who left when the Sandinistas took over.)

During and after the revolution, many Somoza supporters left the country because they knew they would lose their land when the Sandinistas came to power. They were also afraid that the new government would put them in prison. Some were National Guardsmen who went to Honduras, where they began planning a counterrevolution. Others were wealthy business owners who moved to the United States, where they had family or friends. The largest concentration of Nicaraguans living outside their country is in Miami, Florida. A third of the country's educated professionals also left, including 22% of all doctors and medical technicians.

In 1984, the Sandinistas made two years of military service mandatory for all males when they turned 17. Over 30% of the people who left Nicaragua in the past 10 years were students or other draft-age men. The contras set up a network to help draft resistors leave Nicaragua, but often the young men ended up in Honduran contra camps against their will.

The contra war hit the Atlantic coast much harder than the 1979 revolution. Contra attacks along the coast were frequent and violent. About 40,000 Miskitos and Sumos fled to Costa Rica and Honduras. Bluefields was targeted by contras in 1985 and many Creoles left for the United States or Costa Rica.

By 1989, over 35,000 Nicaraguans had returned to their homeland. Many more have returned since then with the help of an agreement between the Chamorro administration and the Honduran government. Even more are expected to go back soon because the United States stopped granting asylum to Nicaraguan refugees when Chamorro took office.

FAMOUS NICARAGUANS

RUBÉN DARÍO was born Félix Rubén García Sarmiento in the village of Metapa on January 18, 1867. He became one of the most famous Central American poets and led the Modernist movement in poetry, which rejuvenated traditional Spanish romantic poems by adding a dimension of expressive rhythm. In 1888, he published *Blue*, a revolutionary and prophetic work that marked the official birth of Modernism. Darío died on February 6, 1916, in Nicaragua.

PEDRO JOAQUÍN CHAMORRO was born in Granada on September 23, 1924. He came from a family that included four former presidents; his great-granduncle of the same name was Nicaragua's first president. Pedro Joaquín studied at the Central American University in Managua and later went to the National Autonomous University in Mexico to study law. His father, Pedro Joaquín Chamorro Zelaya, owned a newspaper called *La Prensa*. When his father died in 1952, Pedro Joaquín became the paper's director. As publisher and editor of *La Prensa* throughout the 1960s, he used the paper to tell the people about the injustice of the Somoza regime. He married Violeta (Nicaragua's current president) on December 8, 1950. Pedro Joaquín Chamorro was assassinated on January 10, 1978, at age 53.

CARLOS FONSECA was born in Matagalpa on June 23, 1936, to working-class parents Fausto F. Amador and Justina Fonseca. As a boy, he helped his mother by peddling the candy she made and selling newspapers on the street. After grade school, he worked for two months before entering secondary school. In 1955, he graduated with a gold medal awarded to the best student each year. He then went to law school at the National University. In the early 1960s, he and two others founded the FSLN. He was imprisoned many times for his involvement with various antigovernment youth movements. He was killed in combat in 1976.

BIANCA JAGGER (pictured above) was born Blanca Pérez Mora Macias in 1945. She won a scholarship to study at the Paris Institute of Political Studies. While in Paris, she met British rock star Mick Jagger. They were married in 1971, but she divorced him in 1979. Now, she is using her fame to boost awareness of Nicaragua's environmental issues. She wrote an opinion piece for the *New York Times* that cut short the government's plan to grant a Taiwanese company logging rights in Nicaragua's endangered rainforest. She has also directed a documentary film about her homeland. As a political activist, Jagger feels the Chamorro government has betrayed the people just as the Sandinistas and Somozas did. She plans to run for the presidency in 1996.

LIFESTYLE

LIVING IN NICARAGUAN CITIES means always being around lots of other people, but out in the mountains and countryside, families might live miles from another house. Some people are very poor, and others are very wealthy. People might support the government, or they may be fighting to change it. For all these reasons, many different lifestyles exist in Nicaragua. But no matter where they live, how much money they have, or which political party they support, all Nicaraguans place tremendous importance on the family.

Certain aspects of Nicaraguan life are changing as the country develops. As a whole, the nation is "behind the times" compared to the United States, Great Britain, and other technologically and culturally developed countries. Part of the problem in recent times is that no political party has stayed in power long enough to establish an effective system of government. The current government is restoring capitalism and a free-market system in an attempt to stabilize the economy. Some people are better off now than they were five years ago, but others have experienced a sharp decline in their standard of living.

Culturally, some changes for the better are starting to show in the country's youth. For example, young people continue their education beyond primary school. They think about race, class, and gender relations and ways to to make their country a better place to live. They appear to realize that they can make a difference in their country's future.

Above: **Like this woman, most Nicaraguans dress in light and cool cotton.**

Opposite: **A boy carries water in a pail nearly half his size. Some areas of Nicaragua do not get running water.**

63

Lack of proper sanitation in some parts, especially in shantytowns, contributes to the spread of disease.

LIVING CONDITIONS

About 60% of Nicaraguans live in cities, and every day many more are exchanging rural living for the urban life. Many people move to the cities—especially Managua—hoping to find better jobs. Currently, eight cities have populations of 20,000 or more. The largest is Managua, followed by León, Granada, Masaya, Chinandega, Matagalpa, Estelí, and Jinotepe. Most cities have well-planned residential areas with gardens, parks, a market, and shopping centers, but nearly all of them also have *barrios* ("BAHR-ee-ohs")—poorer neighborhoods where houses are crowded, small, and close together. You can usually tell how much money a family has by looking at the floor of their home. Poor people have dirt floors, while working- and middle-class people have cemented or tiled ones.

Half the people who are capable of working cannot find jobs, and only 18% have enough resources to meet their nutritional requirements. The country needs 400,000 more houses and apartments to give everyone a place to live, and because the population is growing so fast, an estimated 20,000 more people will become homeless each year unless more housing is built.

The Chamorro administration so far has not made much progress in this area. Many Nicaraguan families build their own homes out of whatever materials they can find—scraps of wood, mud bricks, plastic, wire, rusty tin or zinc roofing sheets, and any other discarded objects that can provide some degree of shelter. They have no electricity or running water, and open drains and ditches serve as plumbing.

GETTING AROUND AND STAYING IN TOUCH

Until recently, only the main streets in big cities were paved. Cars were scarce, and most people got from place to place by walking or taking a bus. Today, Nicaragua has more cars and more streets, but horse-drawn cabs and dirt roads are still very common. Public transportation is fairly cheap, but it is slow and overcrowded. People might have to wait an hour for a bus that is not too full to board. Between 1990 and 1992, the number of cars in Nicaragua

Vendors crowd around a bus to sell beer and candies to passengers.

doubled. The majority of car owners live in Managua, where most roads are paved. Drivers face other hazards, though, like potholes in the roads and frequent gasoline shortages. When service stations run out of gas, it can take several days before they get more.

Finding the way around can be tricky. Neighborhoods have names but most streets do not, so asking directions does not help much. Also, Nicas say, "Go toward the lake" or "Go up" instead of "Head south" or "Go left." While other Nicas usually understand because they know where "the lake" is, these directions often seem vague and confusing to foreigners.

Nicaraguans usually live close to their relatives. It is not unusual for several families living in the same neighborhood to be related. Living close together means they do not have to go far to borrow a cup of sugar or find someone to help carry a heavy load. People help each other out all the time by lending food, giving advice, and doing favors.

Washing clothes is often an outdoor affair, and since there is no running water, it helps if someone pours the water.

URBAN PROBLEMS— CRIME AND SHORTAGES

As Nicaraguan cities continue to grow, urban problems like shortages and crime become harder to control. Electricity and water are rationed, and an estimated 60,000 houses in Managua are illegally siphoning electricity from power lines. Crime, alcoholism, drug addiction, and random violence are on the rise. Crimes against people and property, formerly rare in Managua, have become one of the capital's most talked-about problems. Muggings are very common, so people try to avoid going out alone at night. Car theft is another concern. Even if drivers lock their doors, thieves will sometimes take valuable parts like mirrors, tires, and hubcaps from unattended vehicles. Small children earn a little money by charging a small fee to watch a car until its owner returns.

Several factors contribute to the increase in crime. One is that people who are out of work have a lot of idle time and not much money. Those desperate enough steal food and other items for themselves or to sell on the black market. Shortages also hit people with money to spend. Nicaraguans sometimes walk across the border to El Salvador or Guatemala to buy things that cannot be found in Nicaragua, such as toothpaste, deodorant, underwear, jeans, T-shirts, light bulbs, toys, and makeup. Sometimes, they also go to Costa Rica or Honduras, but the governments in these countries generally are not as willing to let Nicas into their countries.

FAMILIES

The average family has six children and households usually include uncles, aunts, cousins, or grandparents as well. Often, with three or four generations living in the same house, children are indulged as well as disciplined. Parents typically believe that spanking their children or beating them with a belt is an acceptable form of punishment, but mothers and grandmothers are also generous with praise, hugs, and other physical gestures of affection.

Although they place great importance on maintaining close family relationships, Nicas have interesting norms regarding marriage. People do not have to get a license or go through a church wedding ceremony to be considered married. It is much more common for a couple to be considered married because they have lived together for a long time and have children together. This arrangement is called a common-law marriage. It is unusual for a predominantly Catholic country like Nicaragua to accept common-law marriage so readily. Many Catholic societies frown upon women who have children before they get married, but this is not true in Nicaragua either.

Unlike many North Americans, Nicas do not have a negative view of unwed mothers. If a young girl gets pregnant, she is not expected to get married. Instead, her family supports her, even though the Church disapproves. When the baby is born, it is welcomed into the family and everyone helps take care of it. Some girls have babies when they are only 13 or 14, before they are really ready to start a family. When this happens, the baby is often raised by its grandmother while its mother finishes her education.

Nicaraguans look to their youth to build a better future.

67

Woman with child in arms selling bananas to supplement the family income.

DIFFERENT STROKES Boys and girls are treated differently from a young age. Boys are teased and taunted to teach them to be tough, while girls are doted on and treated more gently. When little boys pick up vulgar language, adults are generally amused by it and only punish them if they direct obscenities at adults. Girls, on the other hand, are punished swiftly if they swear. Boys as young as two are given small jobs or errands to do, like going to a neighbor's house to buy ice, but girls are not encouraged to be independent. Even teenaged girls must obey strict rules about going out with friends, while boys are allowed to roam the neighborhood even after dusk.

DOUBLE INCOMES Most Nicaraguan families need at least two incomes just to make sure they can buy enough food. Because it is hard to find a high-paying job, many adults take on two or three odd jobs to supplement the household income. Mothers may work part-time in an office, take in neighbors' laundry, and make candy or *tortillas* to sell on the street. Sometimes, the father or oldest son leaves home to work in the United States.

Children as young as five and six often help out on the family farm or work as street vendors. In poor families, the children must contribute in one way or another just so everyone has enough food. Wealthy families, on the other hand, often have several maids to cook, clean, and take care of the children.

MACHISMO

Machismo ("ma-CHEEZ-moh") defines the power structure between women and men. To Nicaraguans, being masculine means being aggressive, while women's roles are associated with being passive. Men love and honor their mothers very much, but do not treat their wives or girlfriends the same way. They can be disrespectful and even abusive toward women. Because household chores and child care are considered women's work, most men refuse to do them.

Other behaviors, like excessive drinking and getting into fights, are blamed on *machismo*. Many men think cheating on their wives is permissible because it is in the masculine nature, but this irresponsible conduct causes all kinds of problems. Women in several different households may have children fathered by the same man, and often the father does not support any of them.

Mothers today are raising their sons with the expectation to help out around the house and treat women with kindness and respect, but often boys are confused because they still see their fathers acting according to *machismo*. Since the revolution, however, the idea of what makes a "good" man has slowly begun to change. Now, people are defining a good man as one who is responsible toward his family, works hard, and studies to improve himself and his country.

WOMEN AND MEN

Although the current president of Nicaragua is a woman, the country has had a long history of male supremacy. Some people even say that Violeta Chamorro does not really run the country because she has allowed her son-in-law and chief of staff, Antonio Lacayo, to take over most of the presidential power. Women have only had the right to vote since 1955, and today, they are still fighting for equality in a country where being female has usually meant being a second-class citizen.

Until the revolution, women had fewer rights and opportunities than men, but that did not keep them from joining the fight to overthrow Somoza. Three out of 10 Sandinista soldiers were female. The Sandinista government recognized the important role women played in the revolution and vowed to bring about equality between the genders. One of the first actions of the ruling junta was the passage of an equal-rights law.

Unfortunately, laws cannot change certain facts of Nicaraguan life that make women's lives difficult. Spanish culture has a long tradition of *machismo*, an attitude of superiority over women that is shared by most men in Nicaragua.

The authorities know that some men beat their wives, but unless the women report their husbands' violence, the authorities cannot do anything to help. The cultural trait of machismo is so ingrained that some women believe they are inferior to men and see the violence against them as typically male rather than a wrong.

"FICTIVE KIN" AND GODPARENTS

You probably know someone whom you call "aunt" or "uncle" who is not really related to you but is a close friend of your parents. This kind of relationship, called "fictive kinship," is common in Nicaragua. The tradition of *compadrazgo* ("kahm-pah-DRAHZ-goh"), or coparenting, is another way that Nicas use to expand their families and make sure their children are well taken care of. When a child is born, the parents choose a godmother and a godfather, who become part of the family network. They are expected to assist with the child's moral and religious upbringing, as well as his or her material needs. If the real parents should die, the godparents would take responsibility for the child. Godparents are a source of emotional as well as financial and material support. The two families often exchange favors, advice, food, clothing, and child care.

People might ask neighbors, friends, relatives, or coworkers to be their children's godparents, and a lot of thought goes into that decision. Ideally, they want to choose someone with whom their child will develop a lasting bond, but other strategies are also involved. Parents think about all these things when selecting godparents for each child in the family. They choose:

- Neighbors because they can be easily called on for favors.
- Relatives or friends with a lot of money, because they can give their godchildren a financial advantage.
- Doctors, because if the child or anyone else in the family gets sick, the doctor would be able to help.
- Relatives in the United States, because they might send U.S. dollars or items that cannot be bought in Nicaragua.
- Members of the father's family, so that if the father is irresponsible, the child will still get support from the godparent.

HEALTH

Health conditions in Nicaragua are poor compared to more industrialized nations, but they are about the same as in other Central American countries. Diseases, including hepatitis, yellow fever, tuberculosis, and typhoid are all still common throughout the region.

Contaminated drinking water and unsanitary living conditions make it hard to control the spread of disease. Very poor people are particularly susceptible because their drinking water comes from the same streams they bathe in and use for a toilet. Until recently, over half the people who died in Nicaragua each year were children under the age of five. Even today, the leading cause of death among children is diarrhea, usually brought about by drinking polluted water. If no medicine is available, children become dehydrated and lose essential nutrients, which can lead to death.

Though the Sandinistas introduced many health-care reforms, the current government has moved health care down its list of priorities while it tries to stabilize the economy, develop new industries, and privatize the banks. Even without much direction from the government, the health-care industry is becoming privatized instead of being free to the public. The minister of health introduced a plan that gives rural doctors more control over how health care is distributed, but even with this administrative power, the doctors at rural hospitals do not have the resources—medicines, gas for ambulances, or sheets for beds—to provide adequate care.

Another serious flaw in Nicaragua's health-care system is that medicine and supplies donated by other countries and meant for free distribution to the public are systematically redirected to private pharmacies and clinics, where they are sold only to people who can afford the high prices.

Many Nicaraguans in rural areas draw their drinking water from the same streams they bathe and wash in, and this exposes them to the risk of disease.

When the Sandinistas
were in power, they built
schools and provided
children with free and
compulsory education.

EDUCATION

Before the revolution, few children went to school and over half the population could not read or write. Many rural areas had no school. President Somoza knew that by keeping the people ignorant, he was keeping them powerless to effect change. When the Sandinistas took over, they made education a top priority. They built hundreds of schools and launched a teaching campaign that brought literacy rates up to almost 90%. School was free and compulsory for children aged 6 to 13, and two five-hour sessions were held each day to accommodate them all. Desks were in short supply, and some students carried theirs to and from school so they would not get stolen overnight. Students were expected to help clean up around the school. Younger ones picked up litter and washed lunch tables, while older children shoveled mud to release stagnant pools of water, the breeding ground of disease-carrying mosquitoes.

Unfortunately, the contras worked just as hard to destroy these efforts. By the end of the contra war, 411 teachers had been killed. The guerrillas also kidnapped 66 teachers and 59 students, destroyed 46 schools, damaged another 21 and forced the temporary closure of over 550 more.

THE LITERACY CRUSADE

Perhaps the biggest achievement of the Sandinistas was their success in educating Nicaraguans. As soon as Somoza was defeated, the Sandinistas set up adult education programs and vocational and technical training centers. But their pet project was the Literacy Crusade.

Organizers of the Literacy Crusade called upon everyone over 12 years old who had completed elementary education to help teach reading and writing to thousands of illiterate Nicaraguans. Schools were closed to prepare the young volunteers, called *brigadistas* ("bree-gah-DEEZ-tahs"), for the monumental task. In April 1980, after extensive physical, mental, and emotional training, over 80,000 *brigadistas* were ready.

About 55,000 volunteers went off to the mountains and other rural places to teach the *campesinos* ("kahm-peh-SEE-nohs"), or peasant farmers. The rest taught in the cities. In about five months, over 406,000 Nicas learned to read and write.

Because most of the children who volunteered had never experienced life outside the city, the effort became a kind of cultural exchange. *Brigadistas* carried backpacks full of everything they might need. They were sent to homes that were generally several miles apart, and each taught a family or two. The city children were often surprised to find that *campesinos* did not know what televisions or cars were. In addition to teaching, *brigadistas* were expected to participate in the family's farmwork and household chores. Many later reported that the experience was the most inspiring thing they had ever done.

When the Sandinistas were voted out of office in 1990, public education suffered. Today, only three-quarters of 6- to 13-year-olds go to school. The wealthiest families enroll their children in private schools, while the poorest cannot even afford public schooling, as they would have to rent textbooks and pay a small monthly fee. Starting in February 1992, all public high schools charged a monthly tuition fee of $2, while primary schools began requesting a voluntary $1 monthly fee. Several other policies introduced in the last four years have resulted in a shortage of teachers and the closing of many schools.

Graduates of elementary school who can afford to go on to high school and college often enter liberal arts programs, but in the past few years universities have seen an increase in the number of people studying to be doctors, engineers, or scientists. Nicaragua has three main universities. The oldest and largest is the National University of Nicaragua, with campuses in Managua and León. It was founded in 1812 and has more than 22,000 students.

UNESCO (United Nations Educational, Scientific, and Cultural Organization) awarded the Nicaraguan government the 1980 grand prize in literacy.

RELIGION

ALTHOUGH NICARAGUA has no official religion, the most widely practiced faith is Roman Catholicism. About 88% of Nicaraguans belong to the Catholic Church, and the rest are divided among several Protestant faiths. Only a few of the ancient Indian religious traditions remain intact, but superstitions and folk beliefs are common throughout the country.

Over the past 25 years, a new concept in religion, called liberation theology, has emerged in Nicaragua and other parts of Latin America. Liberation theology teaches that God does not want people to be poor and encourages people to try to change their lives.

Opposite: **Church in Jinotepe, one of many in a country where the population is mainly Roman Catholic.**

ANCIENT INDIAN BELIEFS

The religion of the Nicarao Indians was similar to that of the Aztecs. They worshiped corn and natural phenomena like rain and the sun, and believed in several gods associated with these elements. Many American Indian tribes practiced sacrifice, both human and animal, and it is possible that the Nicarao was one of those groups. When they died, their possessions were buried with them because they believed in reincarnation and thought they would need their belongings in the next life.

Other Indian tribes also practiced shamanism, a form of magic. A shaman was believed to have special god-given powers to heal the sick. In some villages in eastern Nicaragua, shamans still practice traditional healing and are treated with great respect. Many Indians also go to shamans to worship their ancestors or to communicate with them.

Although most native Indian religions are now obsolete in Nicaragua, a few vestiges of their traditions remain. Some celebrations, like the Dance of the Little Devils in Granada, combine Spanish beliefs and Indian traditional dances and music. Religious holidays like the Fiesta of Saint Jeronimo in Masaya are accompanied by imagery from ancient religions.

Some historians believe that Indians adapted readily to Christianity because the Nicarao symbol for their god of rain was very similar to the Christian cross.

In Sunday school in church, children sit in the pews to listen to religious teaching.

ROMAN CATHOLICS

Ever since the Spanish brought Roman Catholicism to Nicaragua, the Church has played a significant role in Nicaraguan life. When the Sandinistas overthrew Somoza, they untied the tight knot between government and religion. Some factions of the Church supported the Sandinistas, while others aided the contras. Many of the reforms the Sandinistas were making were too radical for the conservative bishops in Nicaragua. Overall, the church hierarchy resisted change and questioned the authority of the government. With the change of leadership in 1990, a strong bond between Chamorro's administration and the Church has emerged.

In Nicaragua, Catholics believe in God, obey the Ten Commandments, and go to church, but there is also a group of Catholics who think that going to church is not the only way to show one's faith in God. They feel that some aspects of church worship are unnecessarily rigid, and consider themselves Catholics because they live by their interpretation of Catholic morals and values. To them, one of the most important roles of Catholics is helping others less fortunate than themselves. Often, this means going against tradition, but they believe they are still acting as God wishes them to. For centuries, the Catholic Church has tried to maintain a consistent tradition and resisted change. For example, mass was always said in Latin even though few people understood it.

RELIGIOUS FREEDOM

The Sandinistas guaranteed complete religious freedom, protecting the people's right to worship and practice any faith. They also declared that the Church would be an important part of reconstruction. Later the Vatican objected to the progressive reforms implemented by the Sandinista regime, and Nicaragua became one of the key places where the Church fought against liberation theology. The Sandinistas said they were prepared to hear criticism and would allow the hierarchy to voice its opposition, but that collaboration between the Church and the contras would not be tolerated. In 1986, the government expelled Bishop Pablo Antonio Vega from the country because he lobbied in Washington, D.C., in support of President Reagan's $100 million contra-aid plan.

The link between religion and politics was especially controversial during the Sandinista years. Many priests were also members of the FSLN, and conservative Catholics opposed this idea, saying that the interests of the church and the state were in conflict.

While the Church and the Sandinistas disagreed on many things, both groups could understand the benefits of maintaining a working relationship. In 1986, President Ortega and the highest church official, Cardinal Obando y Bravo, held talks to discuss how to proceed. The Sandinistas believed that if they had Cardinal Obando on their side, the public would also support their efforts.

Cardinal Obando was widely respected throughout Nicaragua. In 1987, he was appointed head of the National Reconciliation Commission, formed to improve relations between the government and church leaders. He was also selected to mediate in ceasefire talks with the contras, but he used this position to help Chamorro get elected. He stalled disarmament until after the election to take credibility away from the Sandinistas.

During the Sandinista regime, the Church forced priests who held government positions to either resign from them or give up the priesthood. They also transferred priests who supported the revolution out of poor barrios and into middle-class neighborhoods where the people were less likely to support their progressive ideas.

Religious faith is evident in Nicaragua, and the Roman Catholic Church exerts great influence on government policies.

POLITICS AND RELIGION

Under the leadership of Cardinal Obando, the Church is a principal force behind many government decisions.

When President Chamorro's administration assumed office, its reconstruction plans supported the two main goals of the Church: to create a unified church and to propagate family values. The first was accomplished by expelling priests who held progressive ideas about social reform. The second involved a return to a conservative social order based on Catholic morals. From the government point of view, this meant restoring a capitalist structure in which competition would push people to work hard, while in the eyes of the Church it meant restoring a traditional family structure. The Church believed that women should not work or serve in the military, and were best suited for the role of housewife and mother. This goal held a particular irony in a country under the leadership of its first-ever female president.

Whatever its reasons for supporting the Church's goals, the government helped promote Catholic values. The Ministry of Education joined forces with the Church to create a new school curriculum that reinforced conservative Catholic values, not by teaching the subject of religion, but by infusing the entire educational system with Catholic-inspired virtues. Since the school is the only institution that affects even more Nicaraguans than the Church, it is an even better tool for spreading conservative ideas and values.

THE POPULAR CHURCH AND OTHERS

In the late 1960s, Catholic priests from all over Latin America met in Colombia to discuss liberation theology, a concept based on the idea that God does not want people to be poor or to be treated poorly. Until that time, most Catholics believed poverty and injustice existed because God created them. Poor people assumed their fate was God's will and nothing they did could change it. The priests who believed in liberation theology taught the poor to take an active role in their lives and try to break free from the cycle of poverty. This progressive movement became known as the Popular Church. Two of its early members were the poet Ernesto Cardenal, who became the minister of culture during the Sandinista regime, and his brother Fernando, who became minister of education and headed the 1980 Literacy Crusade. Priests of the Popular Church made their church services more appealing to the common people by saying mass in Spanish and discussing solutions to common problems. Catholic Church leaders opposed the Popular Church movement because they believed God intended for some people to be rich and others to be poor.

Nicaraguan children find church a comfortable and familiar place to meet friends.

The Popular Church is a Catholic organization even though it is not officially recognized by the Roman Catholic Church. Non-Catholic religions are referred to as Protestant or Evangelical. About 12% of Nicaraguans fall into this category. While the Roman Catholic Church is the only religious organization with a strong presence throughout the country (it has a parish in every community), at least 118 different non-Catholic faiths are also practiced. The oldest and largest Evangelical congregation, the Moravian, has many Indian and black members from the Mosquito Coast. The Assemblies of God and Baptist churches are also important in some areas.

RELIGION IN PRACTICE

Nicaraguans are religious people but generally do not frown on gambling, drinking, or promiscuity.

Nicaraguans have a lot of faith in God, but they are often suspicious of priests. The country has a long history of anticlericalism, or lack of faith in the clergy. One reason for this is that historically many of the high officials in the Church and even some of the local priests have been rather wealthy. Sometimes, they were landlords (some still are) who profited at the expense of the poor. People who believe that a good Christian should help out the less fortunate have trouble accepting the Church's opposition to social development programs intended to help the poor.

Roger Lancaster, an anthropologist who lived in Nicaragua for several years, observed that Nicaraguans are highly religious, but not very pious. They are devoted to certain religious beliefs, but at the same time they do not follow all the dogmatic rituals that make a person devout. Lancaster noted that not as many Nicaraguans attend church regularly as he had expected, and that cursing, drinking, gambling, promiscuity, and other activities considered "sinful" by the church are common among Nicas.

In a conversation with a 22-year-old Nicaraguan man named Elvis, Lancaster found an explanation for this discrepancy between theory and practice. "I believe in God, in my own way," Elvis said. "I believe in right living and worshiping God by doing right. Be humble, be honest, don't exploit people." It seems that people in Elvis's country have many different ideas about what is the right way to live, but somehow they all manage to make their various ways of life fit in with their belief in God.

CITY OF GOD

A Catholic sect called the Word of God, which is based in Ann Arbor, Michigan, founded a branch called the City of God in Managua in the mid-1970s. Members of the Word of God and the City of God believe that injustice is divinely dictated and that they have been chosen by God to carry out His will. Their lives revolve around trying to find God and to achieve personal communication with Him. Sometimes, this leads to visions and mystical revelations. Members of the group believe their leaders have great authority because God has spoken to them and told them how to lead their followers.

An interesting characteristic of the City of God is its connection to the government in Nicaragua. The leader of the City of God, Carlos Mántica, is a close friend of President Chamorro, and four members of her cabinet also belong to the sect. Another prominent member of the Word of God is U.S. business tycoon Thomas Monaghan, the founder of Domino's Pizza. He was on the committee responsible for building the new cathedral in Managua (a committee headed by Chamorro herself) and promised to donate or raise half of the $3 million in construction costs for the cathedral.

President Chamorro headed the committee responsible for building this new cathedral in Managua.

CHURCHES

The city of Granada is the best place in Nicaragua to see beautiful churches. Besides the splendid cathedral (above), three other old churches are located here: the Chapel of Maria Auxiliadora, La Merced, and Jalteva. León is the home of an enormous cathedral— one which was intended for Lima and mistakenly built in León—elaborately decorated with many fine statues in ivory, bronze, and silver. The tomb of Rubén Darío, Nicaragua's most famous poet, is also there. The oldest church in Nicaragua—the parish church of Subtiava—is located in León.

The cathedral in Subtiava has a unique feature: a bright yellow sun with a smiling face is painted on the ceiling. When the Spaniards built the cathedral, they included this feature because they thought this would encourage the Indians to come to church as they worshiped a sun god. The Spanish priests hoped to convert the Indians to Christianity once they were in the church.

FOLK BELIEFS AND SUPERSTITION

Many *mestizos* who live in western Nicaragua believe that blacks in the Atlantic region practice witchcraft. While black magic and the "evil eye" are associated almost exclusively with people living on the "other" side, most Nicaraguan men believe *all* women have the power to cast spells over them. Women are said to know how to enchant and bewitch men into liking them, even though most men have never witnessed such a spell being cast.

The tradition seems to be perpetuated by its own built-in factor of secrecy: women never admit to knowing witchcraft but do not deny it either. Men think mothers teach their daughters how to cast spells and forbid them from ever telling the men about it. Women will not reveal whether they know anything about it. In this way, they keep the men believing there is some big secret. The most common spell is the cigar spell. If a woman wants to make her wandering husband come back to her, she should chant a certain incantation over the smoke of a cigar that she must light at midnight.

Other stories and legends from the western region indicate belief in ghosts, devils, and evil spirits. Some people believe that when a mother dies, her soul remains on earth to watch over her children. Her spirit is said to roam the land of the living until all her children have grown old and passed on. The story of Segua, an enchanted woman who roams at night and makes a low whistling sound, is often associated with curses and spells. Nicas believe anyone who sees Segua might have a change of luck. Another popular story tells of people who can change humans into animals because they have sold their souls to the devil. Possession by the devil is usually thought to cause insanity or make people cruel and evil.

Superstitious Nicaraguans believe women have the power to cast spells and bewitch men into liking them.

In eastern coastal communities, folklore is more likely to involve nature and animals. A Miskito legend explains the seasons by personifying summer and winter as two people arguing over whether sun or rain is better for the land. Winter suggested they take turns demonstrating their powers to decide. Summer made everything too hot and dry, killing plants, animals, and people. Winter created rain, then had to stop for a while to let the rain dry up. In the end, they decided to take turns working and resting so there would be a correct balance of rain and heat.

ALDEA S.O.S.
DE NIÑOS

JUIGALPA

◀ BIENVENIDOS ▶

LANGUAGE

NICARAGUANS LOVE TO TALK, and it seems they always have something to say. The official language is Spanish, but a few Indian languages have survived among the Miskitos, Ramas, and Sumos living along the eastern coast. Western Indian languages have all but disappeared, but their influence is still seen in place names and nouns in Nicaraguan Spanish. Many streets, schools, buildings, and neighborhoods are also named after famous Nicaraguans, especially revolutionary heroes and martyrs. The dialect of Spanish spoken in Nicaragua is characterized by a number of interesting expressions, proverbs, slogans, and limericks.

NICARAGUAN SPANISH

The language Nicaraguans speak today is a blend of Spanish, Indian, and Nicaraguan words. Before the Spanish came to the region, the various Indian tribes spoke many different languages. Most of these became obsolete after the Spanish arrived and taught their language to the Indians. Miskito and other Indian languages were combined with Spanish, but eventually most people spoke Spanish.

When the Spanish encountered things for which their language had no names, they adapted the Indian names but often pronounced them in a slightly different way. That is one reason why Nicaraguan Spanish is a little different than the Spanish spoken in Spain and other Latin American countries. Also, most urban Nicaraguans include some English words and expressions that they picked up from North American music or movies. For example, young Nicas say "I love you" in English, and the hip words for money are the English "money" and "cash."

Above: **Mothers of Sandinista war heroes display their own language of love in a demonstration against fighting.**

Opposite: **Directional sign in Spanish, the official language.**

PRONUNCIATION

Nicas speak rather carelessly, often ignoring grammar rules and shortening words or phrases. They almost always drop the "s" sound from the end of words pronounced with an "s" by people in Spain. The often-used expression *Va pues* is one example. *Va pues*, which they pronounce "vah PWE," does not really mean anything: it is like saying "All right, then." Nicas say it all the time. When they momentarily have nothing to say, they say "*Si pues*" (Yes, then).

Another interesting characteristic of Nicaraguan Spanish is the number of words that mean "machete." A machete is a big, long blade, much like a short sword. It is only sharp on one side, and is often used for cutting a path through heavy vegetation. If Eskimos have a hundred words for snow, the Nicas have a hundred for machete. One of them, *machetazo* ("mah-sheh-TAH-zoh"), describes someone who gets sliced up by someone else wielding a machete.

English	Spanish	Nicaraguan pronunciation
hello	*hola*	OH-lah
goodbye	*adiós*	ah-DEEOH
good morning	*buenos días*	BWAY-noh DEE-ah
goodnight	*buenas noches*	BWAY-nah NOH-chay
yes	*sí*	SEE
no	*no*	NOH
please	*por favor*	POHR fah-VOHR
thank you	*gracias*	GRAH-seeah
friend	*compañero*	kohm-pah-NYEH-roh

EXPRESSIONS

Nicaraguan Spanish is full of expressions and idioms. "Walking with the avocados" describes someone who has his or her head in the clouds. Someone who brags a lot is said to think he or she is "Tarzan's mother." Someone stupid and irritating is called *babosos* ("bah-BOH-soh"), which means something like "slimy slug" in English. When people are disgusted, they might exclaim, "*que barbaridad!*" ("KEH bar-bar-ee-DAHD"—"how barbaric").

Two very common expressions in the difficult and shortage-plagued 1980s were *no hay* ("noh-EYE"), which means "there is none," and *la vida es dura* ("lah BEE-dah ehs DOO-rah"), which means "life is hard."

The term *búfalo* ("BOO-fah-loh," or buffalo) describes someone or something strong and robust. If Nicas say someone has a "good coconut," it means he or she is smart, and a dunce is called a *burro* ("BOO-roh," or donkey). Names of fruits are often used in sexual metaphors; for example, a handsome fellow is called a mango. Someone who cannot make up his or her mind is called *gallo-gallina* ("GUY-oh-gah-YEE-nah," or rooster-hen). Children are affectionately referred to as "monkeys."

There are several proverbs that express the idea that everyone has a bout of bad luck once in a while. One such proverb is "Even the best monkey occasionally drops a zapote." (A zapote is a tropical fruit.)

The Nicaraguan saying "Every pig has its Saturday" refers to the inevitable occasional streak of bad luck. It has its origin in the practice of preparing pork on Saturday for a special meal on Sunday.

There are many parts to a married woman's name. In the above example, Anita is the first name, Santiago is her father's family name and Obando is her husband's family name, preceded by the word "de."

NAMES AND TITLES

It is a custom to address people older than you with the respectful title *Don* ("DAHN") or *Doña* ("DAH-nyah"). These words derive from the archaic Spanish words for lord and lady. They are formal titles like sir and madam, but they could also be interpreted as "Mr." and "Mrs." Traditionally, *Don* and *Doña* were also used when speaking to people of a higher social class, and such people were not obliged to return the courtesy. After the revolution, people started to use more informal terms.

Many people also address someone who has published poetry with the title *Poeta* ("poh-EH-tah"). While it is not a formal title, Nicas often use it because they like to treat poets with respect.

In Nicaragua, English first names are common. Spanish names can be tricky to understand because there are different formulas for men's and women's names. Men put their mother's family name at the end of their names, while women drop their mother's name when they get married and add their husband's. For example, former president Daniel Ortega's full name is Daniel Ortega Saavedra—his first name is Daniel, his father's name is Ortega, and his mother's maiden name is Saavedra. An example of a married woman's name is Violeta Barrios de Chamorro. Her first name is Violeta, her father's family name is Barrios, and when she married Pedro Joaquín Chamorro Cardenal, she added his father's family name to the end of her own, prefaced by the small word *de*. Violeta's mother's name is no longer part of Violeta's name.

It gets even more confusing when someone has two first names, like Pedro Joaquín. Speaking informally, people refer to him as simply Pedro Joaquín.

LOCAL DIALECTS

Early Indians communicated by writing hieroglyphics, or symbols that conveyed messages or stories, on special paper made from tree bark.

The native languages of the Indians in eastern Nicaragua shared the linguistic pattern of the Chibcha group of northern South American Indians. Indians in the west, like the Nicarao, spoke languages derived from the Nahuatl linguistic family, which included the languages of the Maya and Aztecs, along with other Mexican and southern North American tribes. Indian tribes in western Nicaragua found it necessary and practical to speak Spanish, giving up their native tongues. By the mid-19th century, only a few people still spoke Indian languages there.

On the eastern coast, some Indians still speak their native languages. The main dialect is Miskito, and some of its words are English. Since the Miskitos have no words for numbers over 10, for instance, they use the English words. They also have a custom of naming their children after whatever they see around them at the time of birth. Supposedly, a man living in Zelaya is named General Electric. Some Miskito words are *tingki-pali*, or "Thank you very much," and *nakis-ma*, which means "How are you?" English is the primary language of most blacks in the region, but Creole—a mixture of English, Spanish, Indian, and black Carib languages—is also quite common.

Hieroglyphics of early Indians.

According to writer Salman Rushdie, a French linguist tried to record the phonetics of the Rama dialect. The attempt was not very successful because the 23 Ramas left were old and had lost their teeth, so they could not pronounce the words right.

ARTS

NICARAGUA HAS a strong literary tradition and is perhaps best known as the birthplace of Rubén Darío, its most famous poet. Poetry is extremely popular, and many Nicaraguans have achieved fame for their writing. The visual and performing arts are appreciated on a local level but have yet to gain international acclaim. Perhaps the most important element of art in Nicaraguan culture is folk art—the paintings, drawings, music, and crafts created by ordinary people. This tradition began long before Columbus sailed to Central America and is shared by most cultures in the region.

RUBÉN DARÍO

Nicaragua has produced more poets than any other Spanish American country. The most famous is Rubén Darío, leader of the Modernist movement that freed traditional Latin American writing from European rules. Darío's vision influenced Nicaraguan writing as well as all of Spanish American literature.

Darío was fond of Walt Whitman, Edgar Allan Poe, and the French Parnassians and symbolists. His poetry was based on ordinary objects, but he used his imagination to elevate common experiences. Much of his early verse described the beauty of the Nicaraguan landscape—the flaming sun, the farms, the pigs and chickens. Darío's poems often associated artistic and spiritual values with Latin America and materialism and false values with North America. Nonetheless, one American, *New York Times* correspondent Stephen Kinzer, described reading Darío as his "most magical and most unexpected" adventure during 13 years of covering Nicaragua.

In Managua, the performing arts center is named after Rubén Darío, and the highest national honor for poetry also bears his name. The neighborhood where he was born in 1867 is now called Ciudad Darío as a symbol of respect.

Above: **Monument to Rubén Darío.**

Opposite: **The folk artist has used the minimum of material for this piece of "rock art."**

"*Darío ... freed Spanish poetry in Spain and Latin America from prosaic dullness.*"

Grace Schulman, in the introduction to a volume of Nicaraguan poetry

Ernesto Cardenal, a priest, poet, and minister of culture during the Sandinista years.

OTHER WELL-KNOWN WRITERS

Almost everyone in Nicaragua has tried their hand at writing poetry, including former president Daniel Ortega. Much of the poetry written in this century reflects the atmosphere of oppression, injustice, and fear that has been present in Nicaragua for decades.

In the past two decades, many women have begun publishing poetry. Before the revolution, most popular poets were men, and their poetry was often political. Much of the poetry written by women has more to do with love, nature, and the beauty beyond the material world.

The Literary Vanguard, established in 1927, was a group of writers inspired by Sandino's determination to drive U.S. Marines out of Nicaragua. The Vanguard's goal was the liberation of Nicaraguan literature from European domination. It was the artistic counterpart of the political desire to free the country from foreign intervention. Joaquín Pasos was one of the early members of the Vanguard. His poetry is filled with images of thought and emotion that reflect the character of life in Nicaragua.

Another *vanguardista* ("bahn-gwar-DEEZ-tah") was Pablo Antonio Cuadra, a very popular author who wrote about everyday life in free verse. He knew Sandino in his youth, and his many poems dealing with political injustice show the powerful impression Sandino's ideas left on him. Cuadra also wrote several delightful pieces about nature that were regarded as brilliant. A versatile writer, Cuadra wrote a drama in 1937, several years before modern theater came to Nicaragua.

Since the 1940s, another great poet, Ernesto Cardenal, has written poems that are probably the most widely read in the Spanish language

Censorship by unstable and repressive governments in Nicaragua has stunted the growth of artistic expression. When he was appointed minister of culture, Ernesto Cardenal encouraged people to express themselves and be creative. He also promoted the rediscovery of Indian arts and traditions. Cardenal wanted to bring art out of the museums, which usually charged admission fees, and display it where everyone could see it, regardless of their social status.

Cardenal also believed that people should learn to play music, draw, paint, dance, and write poetry and fiction, rather than just listen to or look at art. While he was in charge of the ministry of culture, Cardenal helped establish 32 centers for the study and appreciation of popular culture across the country. Many of the centers held workshops and offered classes in arts and crafts. Three major newspapers in Nicaragua responded to Cardenal's call to action by publishing weekly literary sections that included poetry, fiction, and drawings.

Unfortunately, many of the programs the Sandinistas created to further artistic expression have been curtailed since Chamorro took office.

today. Cardenal, also a priest, was appointed minister of culture during the Sandinista years. His first poems were about his love of women, but in more recent volumes, his poems speak of the beauty of natural things and the wonders and cruelties of urban life.

The short stories of Sergio Ramírez contain characters living uniquely Nicaraguan lives, such as a baseball player who faces execution as a political prisoner. Ramírez published a novel in 1984 that dramatizes a series of uprisings from 1930 to 1961; it is a carefully woven portrait of the nation's troubles. Other famous writers include poets Marío Sánchez and Santiago Argüello, and the Nicaraguan-born novelist Hernán Robleto, author of *Blood In The Tropics.*

THEATER

Theater is a relatively new concept in Nicaragua, really only coming into its own over the past decade or so. During the 1980s, theater became a highly politicized form of expression, but since 1990 it has taken a more classical turn. One popular contemporary playwright, Roland Steiner, abandoned the genre of political theater to follow the theme of relations between men and women.

"In Nicaragua, everybody is considered a poet until he proves to the contrary."

—Daniel Ortega, whose most famous poem, *"I Missed Managua In Miniskirts,"* is about the time he spent in Somoza's jail.

ART FOR THE PEOPLE

The National Theater Workshop, located just outside Matagalpa, was very active during the Sandinista years. Directed by Alan Bolt, Nicaragua's most famous playwright, the workshop brought its plays to people in the war zones by traveling to different cities and villages where they often performed on makeshift stages set up in the central park. The actors involved would split up and live among the people for a while to see what problems they were facing. Then they returned to the workshop and created plays based on what they had learned. During the performances, the audience would see themselves in the story and could relate to the situations depicted. This type of artistic expression often helped the people look at their problems in a different light.

"At the beginning I had no idea there was a market for paintings like these, but now we can't turn out enough to meet the demand."

—Maria Silva, a Nicaraguan painter

PAINTING AND SCULPTURE

Some important Nicaraguan artists include the sculptor Genaro Amador Lira and Asilia Guillén, a painter best known for his *Las Isletas* ("lah ees-LEH-tah"), a beautiful landscape of the islands in Lake Nicaragua.

Guillén lived for a time at the Solentiname art colony, where he became friends with Ernesto Cardenal, the poet-priest who helped establish the colony. Cardenal brought paint, canvas, and brushes to Solentiname for the first time and encouraged residents to paint what they saw around them. About a dozen talented painters, mostly women, emerged from the colony. Their paintings are primitive and bright. Some had political themes, while others are beautiful landscapes and depictions of the richness of tropical life.

ARTS AND CRAFTS

The tradition of folk art began with the pottery, baskets, and weaving of the Indians long before the Spanish arrived. The Nicarao Indians created many fine ceramics, metal ornaments, and carved stones. The tribe was known for its skill and imagination in carving jade and other precious and semiprecious stones. The Nicarao traded some of these wares in markets where the standard of exchange was usually cacao. Throughout Mexico and Central America, the Indians produced a variety of crafts, but only a few artifacts withstood the passage of time.

Today's arts and crafts are often made by people who have learned the ancient methods passed down from generation to generation. Thus it is still possible to see how the early Indians might have used their skills and resources. For example, several Indian tribes practiced loom weaving using cotton thread colored with natural dyes made from plants and minerals. They used coal to make black dye, blackberry trees for yellow, seeds of the achiote plant for red, and clay for blue. The hardest color to obtain was purple, which came from an insect living on cactus plants. Today, Indians use synthetic dyes, but they still weave traditional patterns. Another craft that has been around for a long time is macramé, a way of knotting strings or ropes to make decorative designs. The hammock was also created by the Indians, who used little other furniture.

Nicaragua has a ceramics tradition that dates back to the time of the Nicarao Indians.

Two museums, the National Museum in Managua and the Tenderi Museum of Indian Artifacts in Masaya, maintain significant collections of folk and American Indian art, as well as a few pre-Columbian objects.

Dancing and music are very important parts of folk culture. Street performers can be seen in all the major cities, especially Managua. They dress up in elaborate masks and bright costumes to dance, play music, and entertain audiences with skits or songs.

THE NEW FOLK ART

A recent development in the world of Nicaraguan art is mural painting. Murals are large-scale visual stories painted directly on walls, often created by several people working together. Some art experts say that Nicaragua may soon become the world capital of mural art.

Many of the murals in Nicaragua were painted by young people who wanted to express how they felt about their country's political affairs. In fact, most murals portray political messages or stories of historical events that have had a strong influence on Nicaraguans. Try to picture what some of the murals look like:

- A mural covering the exterior walls of a children's library in Managua symbolizes the difference between life under Somoza and life with the Sandinistas in power. One side, painted with dark, cloudy colors, shows children breaking a heavy steel chain that surrounds a high bookshelf covered with dust and cobwebs. The children are reaching up to grab the few books that fall down. The other half of the mural uses bright, happy hues to show children selecting books from an easily reachable shelf and reading them at a large table.

- Another mural shows a woman carrying the blue-and-white flag of Nicaragua and walking next to a man carrying the red-and-black flag of the Sandinista party. It was painted in Granada in the 1980s.

- The largest mural, covering a wall along an entire city block in Managua, represents a series of events in Nicaraguan history.

FOLK MUSIC

While Nicas appreciate many types of music, the traditional sounds of folk music are some of the most appealing. The typical Nicaraguan musical genre is called "Son Nica" and usually contains driving rhythms along with good instrumentals. If you know the Ritchie Valens tune *La Bamba*—or the Los Lobos rendition—you have a pretty good idea of how Nicaraguan music sounds. Along the eastern coast, *costeña* ("koh-STEH-nyah") music is very popular. It is a combination of reggae and calypso.

Some special instruments are used to produce the unique rhythms and melodies of folk music. The *marimba* ("mah-REEM-bah") is like a xylophone, but is made of special wood. Though it has been around for centuries, it is still the most popular instrument in folk music. Other pre-Columbian instruments include *maracas* ("mah-RAH-kahs"), gourds that are dried so the seeds inside produce a rattling sound. The *chirimia* ("chehr-MEE-yah") is a woodwind instrument very similar to a clarinet.

LEISURE

IN THEIR FREE TIME, Nicaraguans like to relax and have fun with their friends. Sports events—especially baseball games—always attract crowds of spectators. People do not just like to watch; they also like to play baseball, soccer, and other sports. When the weather is really hot, families often go to the beach to cool off in the water and have a picnic lunch. But perhaps the favorite pastime is lounging at home. Nicas love to talk, tell stories, and reminisce. Sometimes they watch television, but more often they just sit on the front porch and chat with neighbors.

BASEBALL—THE NATIONAL SPORT

In most Latin American countries, soccer and bullfighting are the most popular sports, but in Nicaragua the national sport is *beisbol* ("BAYZ-bohl"), or baseball. The game was introduced to the country by U.S. Marines in the 1930s, and it soon became more popular than soccer.

Over 200 teams compete at the local and regional levels, and the best ones play in the national championship games. Most cities have baseball stadiums where people go to watch their home team play. The largest one, in Managua, holds 40,000 people. Nicas avidly follow the progress of other cities' teams. Their biggest baseball heroes are Nicaraguans who made it to the Major Leagues: David Green, Al Williams, and Dennis Martinez.

Little boys learn to play baseball by the time they are four or five. Girls play too, but often prefer basketball or volleyball. Children's baseball games take place in fields, parks, vacant lots, or on the streets. Most of them have figured out that a stick works very well as a bat. Some simply use their forearms to hit the ball. No pitcher is needed when they play this way; the batter just throws the ball up and hits it when it comes down. Some children are lucky enough to have a tennis ball to substitute for a baseball, but most use one made out of rags wrapped tightly around a small rock.

Opposite: **Nearly everyone in Nicaragua knows how to play baseball with some degree of skill.**

During the 1980s, when the military draft was in effect, baseball stadiums were frequent targets of recruiting officers. Soldiers would surround a stadium and wait for the game to end. Then, as the crowds spilled out, they demanded proof of registration from all young men. Those who did not have it were immediately taken to army offices.

THE CHANCE OF A LIFETIME

For many Nicaraguan boys, baseball offers the hope of a better future, a chance to become famous. Only a few are good enough for the big leagues, and the annual Youth Pan American Baseball Championship could be their lucky break. Boys as young as seven and eight dream of making the national team and being spotted by professional baseball scouts who attend the games to recruit young talent.

One event, held in Chicago in July 1993, gave a team of Nicaraguan 15- and 16-year-olds the chance of a lifetime. Most of them had never been outside their country, so just traveling to the United States was an adventure. The boys spent two weeks practicing and competing against teams from Argentina, Brazil, Mexico, Canada, Costa Rica, Peru, and the United States.

Alvaro Lopez, 16, started playing baseball in Managua at age eight. When he was nine, he decided he wanted to make a career of the sport. After years of hard work, he became one of the best pitchers in the tournament—he was even approached by the Los Angeles Dodgers and the San Diego Padres about entering developmental camps. He had to choose between that opportunity and a chance for a college scholarship. Lopez and his teammates overcame financial hardships and intense competition to get to the country where baseball was born. Compared to most of the other players, the Nicaraguan team was at a disadvantage because they had been training without the proper bats, balls, gloves, and other equipment. After the competition, the championship committee donated equipment to the visiting teams.

OTHER POPULAR SPORTS

After baseball, the next favorite sport is probably soccer. This game was very popular with the Spanish, who brought it with them when they moved to the New World. Teams for men, women, and children are organized in cities, towns, and villages. Basketball and volleyball are two other common recreational sports, and many cities have established

More basketball leagues are being formed as the game gains popularity among young people.

teams for adults who enjoy a little friendly competition. Junior basketball and volleyball leagues are growing fast because more young people are becoming interested in these sports. Track and field, martial arts, and boxing are not as widespread but are relatively popular. Wealthy people like to play tennis and go sailing. The equipment needed for these sports costs a lot to buy or rent, and most people cannot afford such amusements.

Two popular spectator sports are bullfighting and cockfighting. In rural villages and along the eastern coast, farmers bring their roosters to a clearing where they pit the birds against each other and place bets on which one will win. Roosters have a natural drive to attack each other to defend their territory, and some people find it entertaining to watch. Bullfighting is a traditional Spanish activity that is often part of festivals and celebrations. In Spain, the object of a bullfight is for the matador (the person fighting the bull) to kill the animal, but in Nicaragua the matador has to try to mount and ride the bull. He is judged not only on ability, but also on his style.

A PLACE TO SOCIALIZE

When they are not playing or watching sports, Nicaraguans enjoy just hanging around with their family and friends. In many neighborhoods, people leave their front door open all day so they can call out greetings to passers-by and invite them in for a cold drink. Most homes have front porches where people gather in the evenings to talk, tell stories, and listen to the radio. When it is really hot, everyone takes a chair out to the porch, faces it inside, and watches television from there. Almost all families have a set of rocking chairs—big ones for adults and little ones for kids. Family time is spent on the porch or in the living room relaxing in their rockers. The chairs can be made of carved wood or woven bamboo.

Above: **Adults like to relax in a rocking chair while the children play nearby.**

Opposite: **Talking on the phone is a special treat, because most homes do not have telephones. Every neighborhood usually has a public telephone but callers just have to hope that whoever answers will be able to track down the person they want to talk to.**

FAVORITE PASTIMES

Almost every home in Nicaragua has at least one radio. In fact, for every 4.3 people, there is one radio. This may seem like a high number, but compare it to the number of radios in the United States—two for each person. Nicaraguans listen to music, news, and a variety of political-discussion programs while they do chores around the house and during their free time. In the evenings, some stations broadcast made-for-radio mysteries or soap operas. Many shows from other countries can also be heard on Nicaraguan radio.

You will not find as many homes with television sets in Nicaragua as you would in more developed countries, but people who do not own one usually have relatives or neighbors who do. At 7 p.m. on weekdays nearly

102

STORYTELLING

Nicas love to tell jokes, stories, and limericks. Before the revolution, less than half the population could read or write, so many of these stories were not recorded on paper. Now writers have compiled volumes of stories and fairytales, but many people still know some of them by heart.

Sukling Kwakwalhra ("The Proud Toad") is an old Miskito fable. It is the story of a toad who wanted to go to a party the buzzards were throwing at their house in the clouds. All the birds were invited, and the toad was determined to join them. He stopped a hawk who was getting ready to leave for the party. "I'm going too," he said, "but I'm going to arrive a little later. Would you be kind enough to carry this bag up to the buzzards' house? My bamboo flute is in the bag, and I would like to play it to make the party festive." The hawk agreed. The toad jumped into the bag, unseen by the hawk, and was carried swiftly up to the party in the clouds. There he played the flute all night long. "Ruku, ruku, ruku," the song went. When the party ended, the toad was too proud to ask the birds to take him back down to earth. He jumped into the bag, hoping the hawk would remember the flute. The hawk forgot, however, and the buzzards threw the bag out when they cleaned up after the party. The toad fell down, down, down, until he landed—splat—on a rock. That, the story goes, is why all toads are flat. When the sky is cloudy, Nicas say, you can hear the toads sing, "Ruku, ruku, ruku" for the sun to come out again so the buzzards will have another party.

everyone in the country is parked in front of the tube for the *novela* ("noh-VEH-lah") or soap opera, which is so widely watched that evening meetings are never scheduled for that hour. Only two television stations operate in Nicaragua, but they show a wide variety of local and international programs. Children love to watch cartoons like the Smurfs, Flintstones, and Mickey Mouse. Other favorites are music videos, talk shows, and old American movies.

Not many people can afford to go to the movies very often, but when they have a little extra money, they are a big hit. Even poor families go once in a while as a special treat. All the major cities have movie theaters that show films—mainly ones from the United States—in English with Spanish subtitles. Occasionally, a Nicaraguan-made film will appear, usually at one of a few museum theaters. A movie ticket typically costs the equivalent of 50 cents.

A DAY AT THE BEACH

January to April—when the sun beats down hard almost every day and temperatures rise above 100° Fahrenheit—is beach season. Nicas head for nearby beaches on weekends and holidays to relax, swim, and have picnics. From Managua, it is an hour-long bus ride to one of several beaches. The most popular ones include Pochomil and Masachapa, located side by side on the Pacific Ocean. One of the most beautiful beaches is El Velero, northwest of Managua. The sea is great for surfing and swimming, but it costs the equivalent of $3.50 to get in, so it is more popular with upper-class families and tourists.

Although Lake Managua, Lake Nicaragua, and several smaller lakes do not have pretty, sandy beaches, they do offer other interesting activities. Visitors go to the lakes to row or see the volcanoes, but as the water is

DISCO MANIA

Nicaragua is home to many discotheques, including Lobo Jack, the largest disco in Central America. There are at least six others in Managua and one or two in most other cities. They sport names like Infinito, Pink Panther, and Tom Cat. (Lobo Jack is named after Wolfman Jack, a famous North American radio disc jockey from the 1950s.) The nicer discos have air-conditioning, velvet-lined booths, and real glasses. Beneath mirrored balls, strobes, and colored lights, crowds of young people dance to the beat of Madonna, Bruce Springsteen, and Janet Jackson. The discos almost always play rock music from the United States, with a little salsa and a few Spanish ballads thrown in.

From the disco scene sprouted a new genre of young people in Nicaragua—*chicos* ("CHEE-koh") and *chicas plásticos* ("CHEE-kah plast-EE-koh"), or plastic boys and girls. The term comes from a mid-1980s trend of wearing clothes made of plastic. These were quite expensive, so only upper-class youth could afford them. Now, the expression refers to anyone who wears expensive, stylish clothes. Usually, designer clothes and shoes from the United States and Europe—like Calvin Klein, Sergio Valente, and Nike—can be bought only with dollars, which most Nicas do not have.

Fancy discos are not the only place to go dancing, though. Nicas love to dance, so there are many smaller, less expensive clubs to go to, as well as parties held at schools or under giant tents set up for that purpose.

polluted in some places, swimming is not a good idea. Usually there are playgrounds, ice-cream stands, and historical landmarks near the lakes. Not far from Lake Managua, at Acahualinca, is Nicaragua's most significant archeological artifact. A few years ago, workers digging for building stone discovered ancient footprints left in a patch of dried mud, preserved by a thick layer of volcanic rock and ash. The footprints were made thousands of years ago by men, women, and animals, including a deer and possibly a jaguar. They head toward the lake, and it appears that the people were running, and some were carrying heavy burdens. Archeologists think they may have been running from the erupting volcano.

FESTIVALS

THROUGHOUT THE YEAR, Nicaraguans celebrate many holidays with parades, grand fiestas, elaborate meals, and religious ceremonies. Music and dancing make these events particularly enjoyable. One of the largest festivals is Masaya's Carnaval ("kahrh-neh-BAHL"), or the Festival of Disguises, when people dress up in elaborate costumes to attend balls, banquets, and parades, and to listen to speeches. Carnaval provides a forum for people who do not agree with popular ideas and values to speak out about their beliefs, to dress and act as they please, and to break social rules without getting into trouble. For some people Carnaval means dressing up in disguises, but for others it is a chance to be themselves without fear of criticism. This makes Carnaval a unique Nicaraguan holiday.

Above: **Carnival masks add to the festive mood.**

Opposite: **Festivals and holidays are celebrated with much aplomb, and people wear elaborate costumes to parties and parades.**

Some holidays are religious, like Purísima ("pehrh-EES-ee-mah") and Easter. Some are anniversaries of historical events. Whatever the cause for celebration, Nicaraguans know how to relax and have a good time.

CALENDAR OF FESTIVALS

First Sunday after the first full moon on or after March 21	Pascua (Easter)	September 15	Independence Day
		November 1	All Saints' Day
		November 2	All Souls' Day
July 19	Anniversary of Sandinista Revolution	December 6–7	Purísima
August 1–10	Coming and Going of Santo Domingo (in Managua)	December 25	Navidad (Christmas)

The origin of Purísima lies in the eruption of Cerro Negro Volcano (above) centuries ago. Purísima fun involves giving colorful paper baskets filled with candy. As children go from house to house in Halloween fashion on December 7, they shout, "What brings us so much happiness?" The host shouts back, "The immaculate conception of Mary!" and gives each a basket. No wonder December 7 is called *la gritería ("lah grit-air-EE-yah")*, or "the shouting."

PURÍSIMA

One of the most important holidays for Catholics in Nicaragua is Purísima, a celebration of the Virgin Mary. In most areas, it is celebrated on December 6 and 7, but in Managua the holiday involves a week of festivities, ending with a huge festival on December 7. The tradition of celebrating Purísima originated hundreds of years ago when the Cerro Negro Volcano erupted. It continued to spill lava for days, and the people in nearby León were concerned that it would never stop. Then one day, they took a statue of the Virgin Mary to the volcano and set in down on the smoldering ground. The volcano soon became still. The people believed that the Virgin Mary had saved them from further harm by stopping the activity of the volcano.

Preparations for this holiday begin weeks in advance with several families in each neighborhood setting up elaborate altars to the Virgin Mary. They invite friends and relatives over on the evening of December 6 to see the altars and sing hymns in the Virgin's honor. The altars are draped in fabric and decorated with lights, candles, flowers, branches, and leaves. Each one features an image of the Virgin Mary. Chairs are set up so visitors can stop and pray at the altar. Often, the host gives each guest a cold drink, a piece of sugarcane, a small gift, and an orange before they leave. Because it can be expensive to set up these displays and host large numbers of guests, people take turns at being host, and people who have altars one year are usually guests at friends' homes the following year.

In Managua, the celebration includes an impressive fireworks display on December 7. A big festival is held in some cities, and crowds gather around professionally-built altars to sing. Some families eat big feasts of roast pork and traditional Nicaraguan dishes.

OTHER RELIGIOUS HOLIDAYS

In some cities, like León, *Purísima* is the biggest holiday, but Christmas and Easter are also celebrated with great joy by Catholics. On Christmas Eve, families sit down to a special meal of chicken or turkey. Some people attend Christmas Eve Mass, and at midnight almost everyone goes out into the street to exchange *abrazos de paz* ("ah-VRAH-soh day PAH"), or hugs of peace, with friends and neighbors. Christmas trees decorated with lights and ornaments are not as common as bare branches covered with cotton, but many homes have some sort of Christmas decoration.

Turkey or chicken is served on Christmas Eve, after which the children look forward to gifts from the God Child or their godparents.

Gift-giving at Christmas is common, but most people have little money to buy presents. Younger children believe in the "God Child," a mythical figure who brings gifts, just like Santa Claus. Poor children may not get a gift from their parents or the God Child, but they are almost certain to receive one from their godparents. Even if they cannot afford gifts for their own children, godparents will make sure their godchildren have something to open on Christmas.

Easter, called *Pascua* ("PAH-skwah") in Nicaragua, is usually celebrated by attending church. People visit their relatives. The week before Pascua is called *Semana Santa* ("seh-MAHN-ah SAHN-tah"), or Holy Week. Activities include processions in honor of the crucifixion. On Good Friday, people show respect for Jesus' suffering by going to church or praying at home. The rest of the week, however, is considered a good time for vacationing. The holiday falls at the height of the dry season when it is very hot, so much of the population can be found relaxing and playing at the beach. For sports fans, a popular event is the Nicaraguan baseball play-offs, held annually during Semana Santa.

People dress up for religious processions and almost everyone in the town or village takes part in one way or another.

SAINTS' DAYS

Another occasion for revelry is the day set aside by each town or village for honoring a patron saint. In Managua, "The Coming and Going of Santo Domingo" is observed over a period of 10 days. From August 1 to August 10, Managuans attend parties, hold parades, and watch bullfights, cockfights, and horse races. The main event is a lively carnival complete with rides, dancing, and food. The celebration honors Nicaraguans' Indian heritage as well as their Catholic saint. Church ceremonies commemorate Santo Domingo, but some festival rituals are symbols of the time before the Spanish introduced Catholicism. The music and dancing reflect Spanish and Indian origins.

Festivals honoring Saint Jeronimo in Masaya and Saint Sebastian in Diriamba are occasions for folk artists to exhibit their works. Both cities are known for their beautiful Indian handicrafts. In León, *La Merced* ("lah MAIR-sehd"—Our Lady of Mercy), is a religious holiday. People celebrate by attending church and marching in a procession carrying a large image of *La Merced*.

On November 1, Nicaraguans throughout the country honor All Saints' Day by going to church and praying to the various saints. The next day is called All Souls' Day, a time to remember the dead. For a week leading up to this day, people go to cemeteries to clean up and pull weeds in preparation for All Souls' Day. They also place flowers on the graves of their loved ones. Often they take something that was special to the dead person, like a hat, a bottle of rum, or a picture, and leave it on the grave. On the day itself, families take picnic lunches to eat beside their family members' graves. Many spend the day there, visiting other families.

IMPORTANT EVENTS

The oldest national holiday celebrates the day Central American countries became independent from Spain. Independence Day, observed on September 15, brings colorful parades, fireworks, and speeches to the central plaza in most cities. In Granada, this day is celebrated with much fanfare. Schoolchildren and high school drum and bugle corps march through the streets to the plaza, where everyone gathers to listen to speeches by local government officials.

The Sandinista revolution is celebrated on July 19. People from all over Nicaragua take buses to Managua, where a huge rally is held. During the 1980s, the anniversary of the Sandinistas' defeat of Somoza was a popular time for the Sandinista government to speak out about its plans for reform. Now that it is no longer in power, this day has become a time to remember the many people who died during the struggle to defeat Somoza.

Closer to the home, Mothers' Day is an important occasion to Nicaraguans. Even people who do not live near their mothers try very hard to visit them on this day. Mothers are sometimes honored on this day by being serenaded early in the morning or at night, after dinner.

FOOD

MEALS IN NICARAGUA range from plain and simple to elaborate and hearty, but a weak economy has caused food shortages and hardship for many households. Nonetheless, people are quite generous with food when they have it. When there is enough money, food can be purchased in a variety of places, and a majority of Nicas also grow some of their own food. Cooking at home is much more common than eating out, even though refrigerators and stoves are not found in every home. Restaurants might serve traditional Nicaraguan dishes along with American-style hamburgers, and a wide selection of ethnic eateries can be found in larger cities.

Above: **Busy outdoor market in Managua, where bargaining over prices is a way of life.**

Opposite: ***Pasteles*** **("pah-STEHL-ehs"), a local snack.**

SHOPPING

Anywhere you go in any of the western coast cities of Nicaragua, there is a supermarket relatively close by. Imported goods as well as locally produced foods are generally available. Supermarkets also sell cosmetics, clothes, books, stationery, and pots and pans. Many women find supermarket prices too high for their budgets, so they shop elsewhere. (Shopping for the household is usually a woman's task, although it is also common for mothers to send their children to the market.)

Supermarkets are only one source of food—in any city, Nicas also shop at outdoor markets where vendors sell their goods from individual stalls. Many women prefer to shop this way because the produce and meat are fresher than what they can find at a supermarket. At smaller outdoor markets, vendors walk around with baskets of fruit or other items. A unique feature of markets is the way shoppers bargain with vendors over prices until they settle on one that satisfies both parties.

Some markets are held indoors, but the largest ones take up whole blocks of city streets. One of the biggest is the Mercado Oriental in Managua, where vendors are often lined up six deep along sidewalks and streets. Many items found here are sold on the black market, so they are too expensive for most Nicas. A can of powdered milk may cost five times the regular price because it is not available anywhere else. When necessities are in short supply, people often pay the high prices to keep their families fed.

Some Nicas run a general store, supplying groceries to neighbors.

Shopping for food at local markets is often a daily chore because food spoils so quickly in the hot climate. Another place people get fresh food is at local general stores, which are often located in the converted front rooms of people's houses. Locals know where to go even though most of these stores have no signs. These shops carry staple items and homemade goods like *tortillas*. It is common for people who have refrigerators to buy milk in large amounts and sell it to their neighbors each day. The same goes for people who have ovens—they make *tortillas* to sell to neighbors who do not have ovens.

SHORTAGES AND HIGH PRICES

Finding affordable food has been difficult for Nicaraguans over the past 10 years. During the rule of the Sandinista government, almost everything was scarce. What little food was available at supermarkets was nearly all imported. The price controls set by the government weakened farmers' incentives and caused a drop in local production. The contra war also took a huge toll on local production. Many farmers were drafted into the national army, shrinking the farm labor force. In addition, the contras targeted fields of crops, food storage areas, and trucks transporting food in an effort to undermine the Sandinistas' efforts to raise the country's standard of living.

Coconut trees are commonly found in home backyards.

By the late 1980s, many thousands of acres of good farm land were abandoned because they were in the war zone. Government attempts at rationing food or subsidizing its cost were ineffective because production had decreased so much. The price of food increased so drastically that by 1988, even the maximum basic salary for a worker supporting a family of six would only buy about 60% of what economists call the "basic basket" of essential products. Families had to have at least two incomes, and even then it was hard to make ends meet.

Shortages persisted after the Chamorro administration began in 1990, but since then increased foreign trade and local production have made food less scarce. Today, most supermarkets are fully stocked, but people still cannot afford to buy many necessities. One way Nicas cope with this lack of purchasing power is to supplement their diet with food they can rear or grow themselves.

Most working-class people—even in cities—rear a few turkeys, chickens, ducks, or pigs so they can eat eggs or meat occasionally. And almost every backyard has trees bearing coconuts, bananas, or mangoes.

A *refresco,* consumed straight from a plastic pack, makes a refreshing drink on a hot day. Children often sell *refrescos* on the street or near bus stops, especially in Managua.

COOKING

Like shopping, cooking is usually a woman's job. Nicaraguan specialties often start with *tortillas. Tamales* ("tah-MAHL-ee") are *tortillas* with cheese, rice, hot peppers, and sometimes ground meat inside. They are wrapped in banana leaves and then boiled. *Atoles* ("ah-TOY-ehs") are deepfried *tortillas* with cheese and spices inside. The most traditional dish throughout the country is *gallo pinto* ("GUY-oh PEEHN-toh"), or painted rooster. It is a mixture of red beans, rice, onions, garlic, and seasonings, all fried in a bit of oil until crisp. The name comes from the red and white colors of the beans and rice. Most Nicaraguan families eat it at least once a day.

Two very common beverages are *refrescos* ("ray-FREHS-kohs") and *pinol* ("PEEHN-ohl"). *Refrescos* are made of fresh fruit juice with a little sugar and water added. Locals can usually tell what flavor the drink is by looking at its color: mango is light orange, papaya is yellow, and tamarind is brown. *Refrescos* are sold with crushed ice in a plastic bag tied at the top. People hold the bag in one hand, bite off a corner, and suck the drink out. *Pinol* is a drink made of toasted ground cornmeal mixed with water or coconut milk and a flavoring like cinnamon or ginger. If you mix in some ground cacao, it is called *pinolillo* ("peehn-oh-EE-yoh"). These beverages are commonly served in a hollowed-out gourd.

Vegetables and fruits are frequently eaten raw or used in preparing a meal. Tomato, cabbage, sweet potato, avocado, and yucca are common choices. Fruits can be used to make a number of juices, jams, and sauces. Nicaraguans know how to make a wide variety of dishes out of bananas, including porridge, milk shakes, and cakes.

MEALS AND ETIQUETTE

Corn, rice, and beans are staples in every Nicaraguan home. Fortunate families usually have cheese, butter, milk, and *tortillas* to go with their meals, and once a week or so they have a stew or some other special dish. Less fortunate people might eat only rice and beans. A standard breakfast in a working-class home might consist of two slices of bread with butter (if it is available), an orange or a banana, and heavily sugared coffee. Lunch is usually beans and rice, the leftover bread from breakfast, and maybe a piece of cheese, accompanied by a fruit drink made from lemons or oranges picked from the backyard and sweetened with lots of sugar. Chicken soup may be served instead of beans and rice. A typical dinner consists of *gallo pinto, tortillas,* and fried cheese.

A common practice is the sharing of valued out-of-the-ordinary food items. When someone in the neighborhood prepares a stew, pasta, roasted meat, or other special meal, she is obligated by social norms and customs to share the food with others in the neighborhood. For example, if a neighbor who stops by to chat while you are cooking "helps" by stirring the pot or throwing in a few spices, she should be given a serving when the meal is ready. Also, whoever lends any vegetables, spices, or other ingredients to the cook is assured a sample of the finished product. Nicaraguans believe that you will have bad luck if others see you being stingy, so you have to share with everyone who saw you fixing a special meal—and anyone who even heard you were serving one.

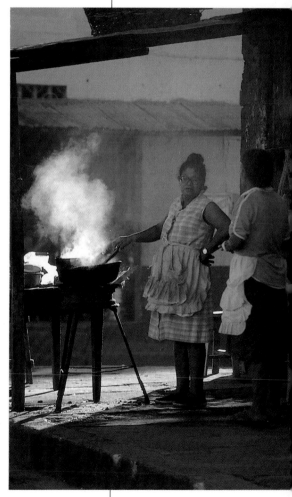

A neighbor who drops by and happens to stir the pot is entitled to a serving of the food.

HOLIDAY FEASTS

In Nicaragua some foods are perceived as being good for you when your body is hot, as when you have been in the sun for a long time or when you have a fever. Other foods are thought to be dangerous to the body if eaten when you are too hot. This tradition of classifying food, especially fruits and vegetables, as "hot" or "cold" is widespread, but strangely enough, the classification varies from household to household.

Meals become an elaborate production during holiday seasons. Women begin shopping and preparing feasts days in advance of Christmas, Easter, and Purísima. Holiday feasts are shared with friends and family, and sometimes the diners can number in the hundreds. Some of the special foods usually reserved for holiday meals are *chicharrón* ("chee-chahr-ROHN," or fried pork skins) and *vigorón* ("bee-gohr-OHN"—*chicharrón* served on a bed of raw shredded cabbage and cooked sliced yucca). An especially prized dish is *bajo* ("BAH-hoh"), a hearty beef or pork stew made with many indigenous vegetables and tubers.

A RECIPE: *GALLO PINTO*

This traditional Nicaraguan dish that everyone in Nicaragua eats daily is easy to make. If your friends think your cooking is "very delicious," they should tell you it is *bien rico* ("bee-en REE-koh").

1 tablespoon vegetable oil
1 small onion, finely chopped
1 clove fresh garlic, minced *or*
$^{1}/_{2}$ teaspoon garlic powder
1 cup cooked white rice
1 cup cooked red beans

Heat the oil in a frying pan. Add the onion and garlic, stirring until brown. Then mix in the rice and beans and cook over a medium flame, stirring constantly for 5 to 10 minutes or until the oil is gone and everything is slightly crispy. Add a few drops of hot pepper sauce if you like spicy food. This recipe makes four servings.

KITCHENS

Aside from the living room, the kitchen is the most often-used room in a typical middle- or lower-class home. It is where families eat, because small houses do not have separate dining rooms. Women wash clothes and bathe babies in the kitchen sink or in a large wash basin kept outdoors. A radio is almost always found in the kitchen because Nicas love to listen to music. Usually the kitchen table is the only table in the house, so children often do their homework there. Upper-class families have dining rooms where meals are usually served. They can also afford to hire maids to cook and clean, and the kitchen then becomes the cook's domain.

Average households might have a refrigerator or a wood stove, but not both. Neighbors often "borrow" each other's kitchens when they need to bake or keep food cold. In the mornings, coffee is brewed not in an electric coffee maker, but in a big pot on the stove. People without stoves cook on two-burner electric hot pads.

A big frying pan is essential, and most kitchens also have several pots in various sizes, enough eating utensils and plates for each family member as well as a few extra, and a large jug for storing boiled water for drinking. Cups and glasses are scarce, so people often drink out of cut-off soda pop bottles with the edges smoothed. A hollowed-out gourd works like a thermos cup, keeping drinks cold even without ice. Milk and juice are stored in small plastic bags that hold one or two servings. Fresh orange juice is served in its own natural cup, made by slicing off the top and carefully cutting away the skin. The spongy white part is left intact so you can hold the orange in one hand and eat it by squeezing and sucking.

Tortillas, **prepared on a hot wood stove, are a staple item during meals.**

RESTAURANTS

Although the majority of Nicaraguans do not eat out very often, there are enough wealthy locals and foreigners to keep even the most expensive restaurants in business. At the Intercontinental Hotel in Managua, U.S. dollars or a credit card will buy an enormous breakfast (about $8) or an all-you-can-eat lunch (about $12). Estelí, Matagalpa, and Managua are three of the best cities for eating out—everything from seafood and steaks to Mexican and Thai food is available. There are restaurants specializing in French cuisine, European dishes, or Swiss desserts. Many Salvadorean restaurants are also found in Managua and León. Two especially good places to get traditional Nicaraguan dishes are El Cartel and Rincón Criollo.

Several vegetarian restaurants in Nicaragua have recently gained popularity. One, called El Bambu, serves particularly delicious and inexpensive breakfasts, including homemade granola. Fast food outlets

"ONE BIG MAC AND A SIDE OF CASSAVA, PLEASE"

Once upon a time, there was a McDonald's in Managua. In 1975, the franchise opened its doors to Nicas who had never before seen the Golden Arches. The establishment also became popular with foreign visitors who wanted something familiar to eat. But within a few years, customers began complaining to McDonald's International (the parent company of McDonald's branches) about the quality of food served at McDonald's Managua.

In 1986, the owner of the local McDonald's received a letter from headquarters that warned, "Do not sell cheeseburgers unless they contain cheese." Well, that was easier said than done in a country where even milk was in short supply. One fast-food competitor in Managua called Sandy's sometimes even sold meatless hamburgers! After the Sandinista revolution, supplies were limited because of the U.S. trade embargo. McDonald's Managua could not import pickles for their Big Macs or the regulation paper to wrap burgers. For a while, the restaurant used Russian wrappers, but customers complained they made the food smell (and taste) like wet cardboard.

The staff used white cheese when there was no yellow cheese, substituted cabbage for lettuce, and when they ran out of french fries, they served deepfried cassava (a tropical plant with a starchy root that is also used to make tapioca). Coca-Cola was rarely available, so the restaurant sold *pitaya* ("pee-TAH-yah"), a tropical cactus-fruit drink.

While the people at McDonald's International were not pleased about these practices, they could not do much about them. To make things worse, they could not even get their profits if they closed down the restaurant because foreign exchange had been cut off. Finally, in 1988, the owner voluntarily severed ties with McDonald's International by changing his restaurant's name to Donald's.

"... a twelve-year-old boy walks by selling shelled peanuts. 'Maní, maní, maní!' Peanuts, peanuts, peanuts! There are a lot of kids who sell peanuts. They sell them on the streets, on the buses, at the bus stops to the people waiting in line, in bars at night. They buy the nuts at the beginning of the day in a giant bag, and then they repackage them into tiny plastic bags."

—*Rita Golden Gelman,*
Inside Nicaragua.

can be quite good, like Rapi Lunch and Soda Metro, or they can be pretty bad. Pizzerias are common, but Nicaraguan pizza is not much like its American counterpart. On the Corn Islands off the eastern coast, there are only a few restaurants, and these serve mostly chicken and chop suey. But visitors are often invited to dine with residents in their homes, and the food served there is tasty. One very unusual eatery in León, called La Merienda, serves an eclectic assortment of meats: iguana, armadillo, deer, and rabbit!

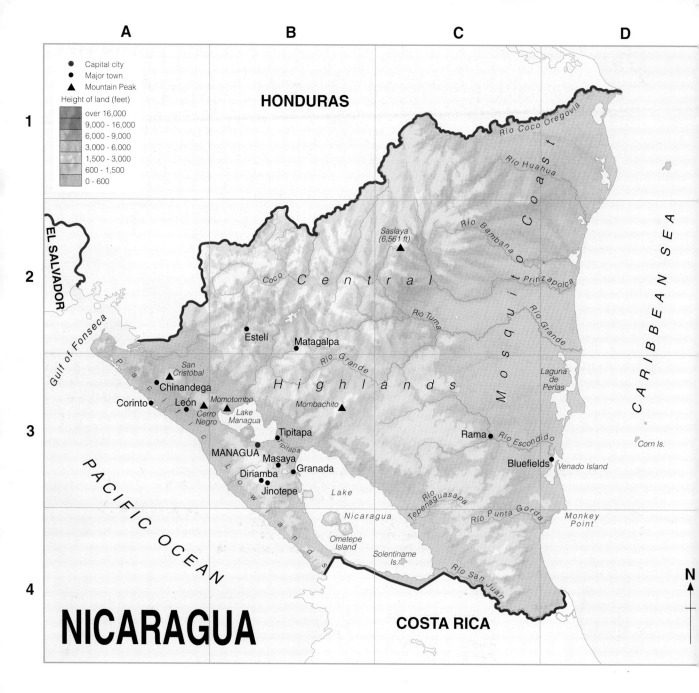

A   B   C   D

HONDURAS

- Capital city
- Major town
- ▲ Mountain Peak

Height of land (feet)
- over 16,000
- 9,000 - 16,000
- 6,000 - 9,000
- 3,000 - 6,000
- 1,500 - 3,000
- 600 - 1,500
- 0 - 600

1

EL SALVADOR

Gulf of Fonseca

Río Coco Oregovia

Río Huahua

Saslaya (6,561 ft) ▲

Mosquito Coast

2

Coco

C e n t r a l

Río Bambana

Prinzapolca

Estelí ●   ● Matagalpa

Río Tuma

Río Grande

H i g h l a n d s

Río Grande

San Cristóbal ▲

Chinandega ●

Corinto ●   León ● *Momotombo*

Cerro Negro ▲   *Lake Managua*

Mombachito ▲

Mosquito Coast

Laguna de Perlas

3

Tipitapa ●

Rama ●   *Río Escondido*

MANAGUA ●   Masaya ●

Tipitapa   Granada ●

Diriamba ●   Bluefields ●   *Venado Island*

Jinotepe ●

Corn Is.

Lake Nicaragua

Río Tepenaguasapa

Ometepe Island

Solentiname Is.

Río Punta Gorda   *Monkey Point*

Río San Juan

COSTA RICA

PACIFIC OCEAN

Pacific Lowlands

CARIBBEAN SEA

N

NICARAGUA

GLOSSARY

barrio ("BAHR-ee-oh") A poor neighborhood.

beisbol ("BAYZ-bohl") Baseball, the favorite sport in Nicaragua.

compadrazgo ("kahm-pah-DRAHZ-goh") Godparents, chosen by a child's parents to assist, among other things, in the child's moral upbringing.

conquistadores ("kahn-KEYS-tah-doh-ress") Spanish conquerors who went to Central America in the 16th century.

contra A counter-revolutionary, someone who opposes the Sandinistas.

dictator A ruler who assumes absolute authority.

fictive kin People who are not really relatives but are so close that they consider each other family.

FSLN Frente Sandinista Liberación Nacionale, or Sandinista National Liberation Front.

gallo pinto ("GUY-oh PEEHN-toh") A favorite dish made with white rice, red beans, and spices fried in oil until crispy; the name means "painted rooster" because of the red and white colors.

guerrilla Covert military fighter opposed to the government, or the clandestine tactics used by such a fighter.

mestizo ("meh-STEEZ-oh") Someone who has both Indian and Spanish ancestry.

refresco ("ray-FREHS-koh") A cool fruit drink served in a plastic bag.

Sandinista Follower of General Augusto César Sandino, or member of the FSLN.

BIBLIOGRAPHY

Forrest D. Colburn: *My Car in Managua*, University of Texas Press, Austin, 1991.
Ronnie Cummins: *Children of the World: Nicaragua*, Gareth Stevens, Milwaukee, 1990.
Rita Golden Gelman: *Inside Nicaragua: Young People's Dreams and Fears*, Franklin Watts, New York, 1988.
Trudy J. Hanmer: *Nicaragua*, Franklin Watts, New York, 1986.
Stephen Kinzer: *Blood of Brothers*, G.P. Putnam's Sons, New York, 1991.
Roger Lancaster: *Life is Hard*, University of California Press, Berkeley and Los Angeles, 1992.
Salman Rushdie: *The Jaguar Smile*, Pan Books, London, 1987.

INDEX

INDEX

INDEX